Things I Did When No One Was Watching

G. K. JOURDANE

BALBOA
PRESS

A DIVISION OF HAY HOUSE

Balboa Press books may be ordered through booksellers or by contacting:

Balboa Press
A Division of Hay House
1663 Liberty Drive
Bloomington, IN 47403
www.balboapress.com.au
1 (877) 407-4847

Print information available on the last page.

ISBN: 978-1-4525-3154-0 (sc)

Balboa Press rev. date: 12/29/2015

Things I Did

When
No One Was
Watching

G. K. JOURDANE

Contents

I dedicate this book to my mother and my daughter. Thank you Joy T and Mary Alvarado for your wonderful support in helping me to get my messages out into the world.

Chapter 1

Forgotten People

It was the early 1990s and just another evening workout at my aerobics class at the local gym. I remember that stormy winter evening well. I headed out of the gym and down the stairs in my leotard, striped leg warmers, and purple headband. What a gorgeous sight I was, heading out of the building into a heavy storm, winds lashing, thunder and lightning having an argument in the sky. I fumbled to put the wet key in the van door. By the time I finally managed to get in, I was soaked to the skin.

I often drove my white work van, which I used for picking up parcels when I didn't have busy days. It saved me from using the heavy truck for a few random pickups. I was a subcontractor for a freight company. It was hard work, but it kept me fit; twice a week at the gym gave me the extra boost I felt I needed. My body loved movement, especially to music with a beat.

As I headed for home, I could hardly see. The wind and rain lashed at the van, blowing the heavy rain straight into the windscreen. Even with the wipers going full steam, I almost had to pull over. The weather was too fierce to relent. I took it slowly until I was almost home.

There was a woman I was about to meet. I knew her only by sight. She was one of those people you see in your neighbourhood for years without ever speaking a word to him or her. I often noticed her on my drive home from work, and she was always alone except for her tiny dog, which she carried in her arms. She was so thin and looked very old and ill. I dare say she probably wasn't as old as she appeared to be. I had always noticed that she had an air of deep loss and loneliness about her.

As I drove around a slight curve, the rain still lashing at my van, I saw the tallish dark figure of the woman walking against the night's wrath. I slowed down, as she appeared to be struggling. She did not have her little dog in her arms. I gathered he had passed away. I drove farther along and then stopped and continued to observe her as she walked past my van. She was struggling to keep on her feet against the storm. I knew something was wrong and feared she would collapse at any moment. I didn't want to alarm her by getting out of my vehicle in the dark. The streetlights were dim and hazy. With the rain, everything appeared shiny, shadowy, and out of focus.

The situation became predictable, of course. She was on her way to a store, but why at that time of night and in those stormy conditions? I decided to drive to the store, park outside, and wait there to see if I could help her. She approached the store, and I casually got out just before she went in the door.

"Hello there. Can I give you a ride home? I saw you walking towards the store, and I'm on my way home from an exercise class. It's a dreadful night, isn't it?" I said with cheerful concern.

She spoke to me in a heavy foreign accent that was very hard to understand. I could see that she was not at all afraid, and I felt she had a history of distant heroic turmoil where she had witnessed horrific things. I knew this was not your everyday woman who had been married and had children and watched them grow up and attend university, delighting at seeing them capped and gowned—the kind of woman who went to cafes and ate cupcakes while sipping tea or coffee. This woman was a living history book.

She told me she was all right and not afraid of people, as I had already guessed. However, I didn't believe she was all right. She looked as if she hadn't eaten in a month. Her hair was like string, and her clothes looked matted, as if she hadn't taken them off in months. She had convinced me she was not afraid of people. Later I was to find out why.

She went into the store to buy cat food, and immediately I thought this was her diet. I felt horrified as my intuition began to kick in. She came out of the shop. I asked her again if she would like a lift home. She was stubborn and assured me she would walk. But before she could refuse my offer of a ride home again, I reached down gently and took her bag of cat food from her hand. Then I opened the door of my van and helped her up into the seat. She just looked at me with hardly any expression. Her eyes were glazed over, small and sunken. I could see she was not capable of doing much for herself.

I started the engine and then turned to her. I put her seatbelt around her. She was so thin that I couldn't get it to fit. It remained loose. Just as well—we had a short drive.

"I'm Rikki," I said. "I live just down the road a bit. What's your name?" Taking my eyes off the road for a second, I glanced at her with a gentle smile on my face.

"Margo."

"Are you German, Margo?"

"No, but you are, Rikki."

"Well, no, I'm not really. You see, my father was a soldier. He fought and killed many Germans in the war, and he named me Rikki as a mark of respect for the men he killed."

She nodded her head slowly.

"I have not an ounce of German blood in my veins, Margo. My father came back from the war a damaged and extremely fragmented man. I know much about the lives of soldiers and why they fight uselessly, only to end up a mess."

A lot of men in those days had no choice but to fight for their countries. My father left for the war at sixteen. He'd had no idea what he was doing. He was just a boy. He often told us it was a way of seeing the world, and I assume a lot of young boys who grew up in the poorer parts of town, such as my father, had that same idea. In some ways, war is innocent. Men don't know what they're fighting for.

Margo was quiet. I suspected she had not much energy to speak. It seemed she was gazing into the distance, into some unseen world, even as she looked at me. It was as if part of her were seeing from another place, another time. She was completely unafraid.

"You are certainly German, then," I said.

"Austrian. My husband died two years ago. I miss him very much. I don't know what to do now that he's gone."

I said nothing as I drove slowly, nodding my head as she continued to ramble. When we feel deep emotion and have no words to express something, or following an in-depth conversation, we nod our heads. Or maybe it's from boredom, though I was definitely not bored with Margo's words. I wanted to know everything about her life, starting when she was born. I was fascinated and sad at the same time. I didn't know what to say to her. I was already very touched by this dear soul.

"You can just drop me here," she said at last.

"Which house is it, Margo?"

"I'm all right to walk. Just let me out here."

I pulled the van over to the kerb, got out, and opened the door to help her. The rain had ceased. The road was quiet and sullen; the streetlights reflected in the puddles, giving off an eerie shimmer. As we walked, Margo talked more, telling me about her days as a dancer during the war. She had not had children.

I stopped walking and asked her where her house was. She pointed in the direction of a gate. She didn't want me to go inside.

I asked her about the cat food, and she said that it was to feed feral cats. I knew she was consuming it herself. I also knew I had to come to see this woman again.

Margo seemed to want to keep talking, and I wanted to allow her to continue. Her rambling had hooked me into an abandoned era. But I was beginning to feel tired, and I needed to get warm. I left, promising I would come back to visit her in a few days. I was busy with work, though, and returned a week later, on a Saturday afternoon. I knocked on her door, and there was no reply.

I banged hard a few times. Still nothing. I peeped through the mail slot in the door, and I was shocked by what I saw. I could see the kitchen down at the end of the hallway and part of the lounge; they were bare. I shouted through the slot, hearing my own voice echo into the emptiness. I knew she had gone. It looked as if no one had ever lived there, and it seemed as if Margo had just been a ghost.

Standing there puzzled on the veranda, I eventually started towards my van. That's when a middle-aged woman came running out from the house next door.

"You're wondering about Margo? She's been taken away," the woman said.

"What do you mean? Where to? I'm so sorry. I'm not a friend of hers. I gave her a lift home a week ago, and I just stopped by to see if she needs anything." I felt dread and was prepared for the worst news. "So is she in hospital?"

"No, she's been taken into care."

"You mean a rest home or something?"

"Come with me." She grabbed my hand, pulling me towards her house. "Your name is …?"

"Rikki."

"Helen. Nice to meet you. Let's have a cup of tea. Come on. I'll tell you all about Margo. I've lived next door to her for many years."

"Please tell me where is she now. I must visit her." I was impatient to find answers about this mysterious woman I had found wandering on a stormy night, the woman I had seen in broad daylight for such a long time prior to that, a little dog in her arms.

As we sat drinking tea, I said, "Tell me all about Margo. She told me she was a dancer, and that's about all I know."

Helen got up from her chair and took a book off her china cabinet. "Here are some photos she gave to me before they took her away into care. She was a royal ballet dancer and quite well known in Europe in her day. She came out here with her husband after the war, and no one knew who she was. Her family had been taken to Belsen, where they died."

I didn't tell Helen that Margo had already told me that. "What about all the cat food? Is it true she has all these cats to feed?"

"No, she only ever ate cat food. I tried to help her, Rikki, but she refused everything I offered her. It's as if she has a death wish. She lost her zest for life after her husband passed away."

I gazed at the photos, not able to put the woman I saw there and the woman I knew together in my head. She had been elegant, like a swan. *How did this person come to be like she is?* I asked myself. I began nodding, as I usually did when feeling overwhelmed.

"When they came to take her," Helen said, "she started talking in Austrian. She thought it was the Nazis come to take her prisoner."

I just sat nodding my head and staring down into my cup of tea. "Where can I visit her, Helen?" I asked quietly.

Helen rose again from her chair for a pen and paper. She gave me an address of a nursing home in Devonport, half an hour away from where I lived in Auckland. I knew then why, after what Margo had been put through in her life, she was no longer afraid of people or of walking in the dark alone.

Weeks passed, and I got on with the usual things, like working, seeing friends, keeping fit, and so on. But I still thought about Margo and the photos I'd seen of her, not to mention Helen. I had the address she had given me crumpled up in the pocket of my jeans, and one Saturday I randomly jumped into my car and drove to the address. It was easy to find. It was a fine hot day; the sky was so blue, and I felt enthusiastic about life and full of anticipation. When I arrived to see Margo, I didn't know what to expect. Would she still recognise me? I had stopped on the way to buy her a beautifully wrapped box of biscuits.

The nursing home looked like a huge English-style white cottage, with a turret and lovely gardens displaying a feast of colours. Carnations, busy Lizzies, and hydrangeas graced the narrow pathways that led to an open doorway, reflecting my zest for life.

I heard music coming from inside the home but saw no one. It felt rather ghostly as I walked in without knocking.

"Hello?" a voice said, and an old man appeared.

"Is Margo about?" I asked.

"Margo... Margo," he mumbled. I followed him; he pointed to a room where the door was half-open. I nodded and walked in carefully, as if on eggshells. The music had been turned off. There was Margo lying on a bed, looking at the ceiling.

I placed my hand on her head and leaned over and kissed her on the forehead. "Margo." I spoke in a whisper. "Remember me? It's Rikki." I explained that I was the person who had given her a lift home from the store on that stormy evening. Then she remembered who I was.

She put her hand out for me to hold, still gazing at the ceiling. The floor's carpet had faded, the flower pattern almost threadbare. The walls were wooden, and a noisy fan whirred on the ceiling. Below it hung a three-tiered carriage light with a slight film of dust on it. Margo didn't seem to see it. It was as if she were looking right through the ceiling and the lights and fan didn't exist.

Her face was terribly gaunt and pale. Her eyes were sunken. I knew death was in the room that lovely day.

Suddenly, she turned her head toward the biscuits I had bought for her. I opened them, and she insisted I have some, but she said she didn't have an appetite at the time. She began telling me where she had things stashed away so no one could take anything.

"People steal your stuff in here," she remarked.

I sat with her for half a day. I combed her thinning hair, and we talked, but not about anything in particular, as her mind was failing. I was just there so she didn't feel abandoned.

"I'm tired of looking at that closet. It follows me everywhere," she whispered.

"Yes, I know." I knew what she meant by this. You get used to the look of things; they become familiar and comforting to you, like your bed. A mark on the ceiling can be a comfort after looking at it for so long. I knew this from the depression and sickness I had suffered in recent years. Even a hole in a floor can become a familiar comforter to a suffering person, before he or she becomes tired of it.

In a while, I knew it was time to leave Margo. I'd probably never see her again after that day. I took off a crystal I wore around my neck, put it in her hand, and closed her fingers into a fist. "I want you to take this. I don't need it anymore."

She was too weak to argue about it. She looked at me and touched my hair. I sat for a long time, holding her hand between my hands as she looked up at me from her bed. We exchanged unspoken words in those moments. I knew that we both felt love. We understood each other. I felt great empathy, and she knew that too.

"I'll come back and see you next week." I bent down and kissed her forehead for what was to be the final time. My hands slowly left hers. She once more lay staring at the ceiling that had become so familiar to her already. I never went back.

There is always something different about people like Margo. I was very privileged to have met someone as brave, strong, and noble as she was. Margo was a living affirmation that I was fortunate enough to have met through an act of compassion on a stormy night. Her strength has inspired me through the decades. It was not what I did for her but what she did for me that had a lasting effect.

Twenty years have passed, and I think of her often. Margo rests in my heart's memory—the private place where we keep all our secrets.

Chapter 2

The Butterfly Messenger

It was the middle of an Australian summer as I walked into the hospital with my mother to take her for a scan. I was scantily dressed in a pair of white shorts that were frayed on the ends and an almost see-through yellow crop top. I was fit, healthy, suntanned, and aware of my slow pace while escorting Mum down the long corridor. We sat down to wait. She got up when she remembered to check in at the desk. We both sat reading until she was called in.

Mum put down her magazine and strutted in for her scan quite confidently. I continued to flick through the pages of mine with an uneasiness in the back of my mind that the results of her scan might show something life threatening. I glanced up; I was the only person there. The magazine lay resting in my lap as I began thinking aimlessly.

The nursing staff and doctors with stethoscopes bustled past the waiting area, eyes fixed ahead, their expressionless faces seeming to indicate the importance of their professions. It was hard to imagine that there was a sunny, bright day outside, and I wondered how people could work in such dismal surroundings, with fluorescent lighting all day, without going crazy.

I was hoping Mum's scan would be clear. I felt a twinge of panic, but it was controllable. Suddenly, a bang broke the silence. A woman in a wheelchair headed down the corridor, pushed along by her apparent carer. To avoid making her feel awkward, I glanced away as she approached the waiting area.

The carer left her to wait while she went off elsewhere. We were the only two people sitting in the silence of that place. She caught me briefly looking at her; she smiled, and I nodded and smiled back at her as if there was an unspoken respect between us. I looked at her when I felt she was not aware. She wore a pink dressing gown with matching slippers. She looked around fifty-seven years of age. I began to wonder what her life had been like before she had become so ill. I felt sad and wondered why life was so fleeting and unfair. There I was, young, fit, and healthy, and I began thinking about my own mortality and where my life was headed.

I had to go check the meter box outside, as I didn't want a parking ticket. Just as I stood up, the woman began getting out of her chair. I went over to help her up and asked if she needed the bathroom.

"No, I'm fine, really. I want to stretch my legs a bit." She walked slowly with me down the corridor. I felt as if I had known this woman for years. There was no awkwardness, and our conversation flowed. I had made a new friend. We had almost reached the double doors, and it seemed as if hours had gone by. I asked her if she wanted me to walk her back to her wheelchair.

"I'm not the least bit tired right now," she said, "and I don't get a chance these days to talk to anyone much, only when my family visits me."

I suddenly remembered the reason I had gotten up from my chair. But I didn't care about the meter box or about getting a parking ticket. We continued to talk about life, and I wanted to hear more about hers. We spoke of her children and how times had changed so much. She said her life had been so wonderful, and she would not do a thing to change it if she had to do her time over. She mentioned how lovely and fresh I looked and asked me if I was a tennis player. I felt both saddened and humbled.

I hadn't noticed that Mum had already begun walking down the corridor towards the doors where I stood with the woman. It was time for us to leave. I glanced down at the woman She wore a clear plastic medical band with her name and the word "hospice" on it. I didn't know what to say to her. I knew I would never see her again. This person had just shared a part of her life with me, and I would never be in this place again, talking to her as I had just done.

I knew that she knew this too. We looked at each other, and we hugged. I felt I wanted to go with her to wherever she would go eventually. I felt the quicksand feeling of hopelessness for her, of not being able to put my hand out to save her from her fate. Oh, how I wanted to with all my might. But her mortal time had run out. I didn't know what to say. I wished her all the very best but felt inadequate saying this to a person who was moving on from this earthly realm.

Mum approached, and I allowed her to go on slightly ahead of me. I turned back and puckered both lips as I looked directly into the older woman's face for the last time. Mum and I had reached the door, and I gave a final wave before it closed. Outside, the sun was hot, and I was expecting a parking ticket, but much to my surprise, I had been lucky. My body felt good being outside again, only I felt as if I had just lost a friend.

A month passed, and I still thought about the woman in the corridor, wondering if I should call the hospice. I phoned and explained who I was and the circumstances in which I had met her. I asked if I could send her a parcel, and they said that was okay. A few days later, when I was out shopping, I found the perfect gift to send. In a shop doorway stood a box of different coloured butterflies of all sizes. I was instantly drawn over to the box. I gently began picking some up and wondering what colour she would like, realising I had no idea what her favourite colour was. Suddenly, it dawned on me: the day we spoke she was wearing pink. That had to be it. I saw a lovely card with a pink butterfly soaring upwards into the sky.

I went home and carefully put the butterfly into a pink box along with a card with a special message I had written inside it. I had it sent to the hospice. After one week passed, I decided to call the hospice to see if she had received my gift. I was informed that her daughter had received it. She was so delighted indeed that a stranger cared so much. I thanked them. I put the phone down, knowing she had passed away.

Many years went by. I became older, my hair slowly turning grey, and I wore my shorts a little longer. I was not very fit and had health issues. Upon seeing a pink butterfly somewhere, I think of that day in the corridor of the hospital.

I awoke one morning feeling unwell and decided to head out to clear my head. I drove to our local cemetery, where I had often sat in its serenity. In strolling through the graveyard and reading the names on the headstones, I looked about at the lovely fresh flowers, noticing that some had withered up. It was obvious that some of the dead had been forgotten. I heard the noise of traffic in the distance, reminding me of life moving by and that one day we may be forgotten. I began to question the importance of life itself. Was there truly a god? Perhaps. I did not have the answer to what happens beyond the grave.

I kept strolling and then paused for no reason. I turned around and looked down slightly. My eyes fell upon a name on a headstone, and I knew straight away. I knelt down beside it, knowing I had found my friend. I laughed aloud and began talking to her, filling her in on my life, from where we had left off in the conversation we had that day in the hospital corridor.

I felt a little silly talking to a headstone, wondering if someone may be watching me.

There was the date of her passing, and this would have been correct. There were two little yellow roses in a small vase on her grave. I went back in a few days and placed a pink butterfly upon her grave.

Chapter 3

New Light through Old Windows

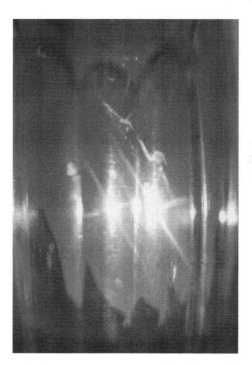

After leaving Queensland because we were unable to find a suitable house to rent, we headed for Melbourne, where Mum and I ended up homeless on the outskirts of the city of Melbourne. She was seventy-eight, and I was fifty.

After spending many days and nights in our old car, we managed to stay with some friends before we outstayed our welcome and had to move on to rent a condemned old house. We covered ourselves in our dressing gowns that we used for warmth in the dead of winter. Coming from a tropical climate, we had very little heavy clothing. We lived on snippets of junk food purchased with coins I scrounged from obscure places inside my car.

I worried about Mum, as she was seriously ill with cancer and had not long been out of the hospital after having a mastectomy. I was unable to conduct my therapy business due to my certificates being outdated. Seeking new ones in the field I was qualified in was impossible, as it would take weeks or maybe months.

I would have to work another job and take care of my ailing mother at the same time, but no matter how I tried, I was unable to get work anywhere.

We had been struck down with horrendous coincidences, and I knew I had hit rock bottom. Mum seemed stoic for my sake, but it didn't help.

Here we were, along with two lizards who also seemed to be stoic. I was falling apart inside. I had run out of ideas and eventually hope. I felt the life draining out of me; I was running on empty. We were near the town of Mornington Peninsula, on the outskirts of Melbourne.

I had been a sports therapist for years and never had a problem with running a business from home until now. I had been required to obtain legal papers, I couldn't imagine what all this fuss was about. I began filing out the questionnaire, as I kept going down the page, some of the questions were becoming disturbing to me, wanting to know if my job as a therapist involved any sex on the premises.

This was absurd.

Tearing up the papers, I began kicking the pieces all over the floor, swearing and cursing my whole life. This upset Mum, and she took a turn for the worse. I didn't know where the emergency clinics were located. My mind was a total blank.

In a state of panic, I called an ambulance. My heart was banging in my chest from rage and now the fear of losing my mother. Things were a mess. I had an anxiety attack. I felt it creeping through me like a horrible curse, and my head started spinning. I felt as if everything had become surreal. I was locked in a tiny barrel, trying to escape. It was crushing me to death.

I felt so sick.

Staggering aimlessly into the backyard and looking up at the grey sky, which was spinning around as I groaned and tried to talk to God or anyone who would listen, I wandered into the neighbour's backyard, holding my head.

I vaguely remember a woman talking to me. It was if I were in a drugged state. I fell on the grass holding my head, talking to her and not knowing what I was saying. I felt as if I were in hell and wished for death to take me away from this pain. I was disorientated in my consciousness.

Things were a complete jumble inside my head, causing me to lose the ability to make decisions. Anxiety attacks became almost an everyday occurrence from then on, making me resort to taking Valium once again to help me cope with my existence.

I was thankful for the clients who came to me from the very first advert. It was all we had to rely on for income. The movers had just brought our furniture in from storage, and we had gone to the bother of unpacking it all before I had that terrible phone call saying I could no longer advertise.

As I found, the structure of renting is vastly different from what it used to be when I was a teen. First you call your real estate agent about the house you want to rent, and then you show up when they have an open home. The owners of the property then goes through the names of all the perspective wannabe occupants and decides who they want living in their house.

We had above average references, yet we were unable to get a place to live, making us "homeless." I found this insulting and degrading to my very core. We were not used to renting and did not know the pitfalls.

After trawling through pages upon pages of real estate sites for hours in an Internet cafe, I finally found a suitable place, but was it to be? After all, we had left Queensland because we had nowhere suitable to live. We had felt unsafe living in a drug-ridden area where there were burglaries every day and noisy cars drag racing around the streets at all hours of the day and night.

I called the agent and explained our situation. They were happy to take a bond and three weeks of rent in advance. I was relieved. My question to fate is this: why, when we had gone through all this hardship in Melbourne, was it so easy to get a place to live this time? Was there a lesson I had to learn from this horror of homelessness, no money, and our entire time spent just surviving? Mum used her pension money to carry out this ordeal so we could secure the place we were to return to in Queensland.

Our friends had made the best efforts they could under the circumstances. They were kind and caring, and we loved going to see them. It was hard even to open the door of that horrible house after spending time at our friends' lovely upmarket villa.

The rental was expensive, and I felt relieved that I could pick up where I had left off, working from home as a therapist with my faithful clientele. It was a quiet, leafy neighbourhood, and I needed the peace after such a traumatic time in Melbourne. Work, as usual, was busy; often I worked into the evenings.

Four months passed, and I received another phone call that would send me back to hell again. Company crooks had taken our investment money. It was gone completely, along with my future plans, shattered like pieces of glass hitting a concrete floor. I was in a state of shock and complete disbelief. This caused my mother great anguish, and again anxiety made itself present in my life. It meant I would have to rethink my retirement plans. Taking my own life seemed the best option, as the bad stuff just kept happening. I had completely lost everything this time; I felt hollow, and severe depression was beginning to set in. This was the second investment we had lost through skulduggery. How much more could one individual take?

The loss of my investments was not my mistake. It came about through the deceitful actions, lies, corruption, and dishonesty of those I had entrusted to keep my finances safe. More than one million people had their life savings in this investment, and I soon learned that others had actually succeeded in taking their own lives.

Ain't Loneliness a Bitch?

As the years continued and my depression worsened, I thought of ending my life several times. I began having problems with my health. I developed chronic fatigue syndrome, finally resulting in an autoimmune disease. I forced myself to go on living. I began working weekends to earn extra money to save for a house of my own, where I could finally settle and live normally, and to book myself into a health retreat. Sadly, I never got to experience the joy of either. I always needed the money for something that was happening. It felt as if my life had been cursed. Everything had come to nothing. My plans and goals shattered before me, and Mum and I were broke, with only enough to pay the weekly rent. Days, weeks, and months were flying by, turning into years. I continued to work random hours despite my failing health.

The Black Hole

Two of the men in the company responsible for the theft of all the money were tried and jailed. One was the company's lawyer, the other the executive director. The third was the main shareholder of the company in question and had fled into the night. Things were a mess.

Meanwhile, I carried on. My mother seemed stoic, as she always did.

"Oh, trash night again," I mumbled, and then I sighed. I had become very irritated and tired. The days were long, tedious, and lonely. I didn't feel the same about my life anymore; I had lost faith in humanity and my trust in people. I began hating the world and everyone in it.

As I hauled the wheelie bin down to the gate, I looked around at the evening sky and breathed in the crisp air. *Why do these things happen to me?* I became obsessed with this thought as I continued on autopilot. I reached the bottom of the gate.

"Friggin' bin," I mumbled to it, as if it could hear me. I felt a tired anger deep within. My body was exhausted; the investment crash was constantly in the back of my mind, and it brought me a feeling of sick black doom, like a shadow that clutched at my very soul, affecting whatever future I'd had.

I continued mumbling to myself as I walked up the driveway. I noticed our neighbour as I passed by her window. I had never seen her until then. She was a frail woman of eighty-three, and her name was Mabel. She had a large hump on her back, and she stood stooped over, like a letter *c*. Her head pointed almost directly at the ground.

Ouch, I thought. Her condition looked very painful. I had noticed she never had visitors except for someone in a black sports car who would show up on occasion. This was her grandson, Greg. Mabel had become unpopular in the complex of townhouses.

Sunday morning came again, and I did some washing. As I was hanging it out, a tiny hand appeared through the crack in the wooden panelling of the fence that separated Mabel's townhouse from ours.

I couldn't see her face, but I heard her frail voice. "I'm your neighbour."

"Hi. I'll come over and introduce myself properly next week if you like," I replied as I shook her cold little hand. She didn't reply, and I heard her shuffle off.

I decided to go over that same day to get the neighbourly introduction over with, as I knew I would get busy with work the following week. I was becoming a social introvert, only on a mission to make money, as I had been robbed of my retirement nest egg. How I was going to get on in the coming years? Both my mother and I were flat broke and had only some small savings left.

I felt sombre and couldn't be bothered to go in and see Mabel. I had nothing that would interest her. I didn't want her asking me questions and to have to put on a cheerful mask while I made up lies about my situation. I was irritable, not wanting to talk to anyone except the clients who came to see me daily. After my workday was done, I would shut myself off from everything and lie on my bed upstairs, just existing.

Afternoon came. I took a few steps from my front door to my neighbour's. The door was closed. I tapped gently, and it took a while before she opened it. I heard the locks undo, and there stood this woman, bent right over, as I had seen through the window earlier. She was so short that I had to bend down in order to hear her.

She told me about her grandson and her only daughter, whom she had no contact with as a result of a family feud. Mabel had broken her back, which explained the large hump; she had also suffered several heart attacks and had trouble breathing. Her house was impeccable. She had a woman come in once a week to tidy up and shower her.

Mabel seemed concerned about her trash.

Oh, not trash again. Those bins and the nutter who has an obsession with lining them up like soldiers on trash night, I thought. Fred, who lived opposite me, was a cranky old bugger to everyone. I found out years later that he suffered from mental illness and had become obsessed with the wheelie bins and the complex. I had already had words with him over the bins upon first arriving from Melbourne, and it was obvious he did not like Mabel one bit.

I offered to take her trash bin down once a week for her. She was so relieved and grateful.

"It's no bother, Mabel," I said. "I have one free hand for yours." I joked.

As time moved on, I saw her often, and I called to see how she was. I was good at comforting the lonely; perhaps it was because I was lonely too. After all, I had arrived back in Queensland broke, and then our nest egg had been ravaged by company rogues. My car was a wreck, my health was going downhill, and my mother needed me to care for her.

I saw ambulances arrive many times to take Mabel to a private hospital. One time I found out she had not been eating. In her pantry, I found packets of chips and biscuits. There was nothing to speak of in her fridge or freezer.

Where's her family? Why aren't they playing their part? I wondered. I became angry at their irresponsibility. I was a complete stranger, yet having to do what her family should have been doing.

I drove to the hospital to see her, as I knew she would not have one visitor. The hospital was a terrible place—badly designed, small, and having skinny windows with no views. It resembled an igloo. The medical staff seemed offhanded and uncaring. The place was surely a fire trap, and to top it all off, there was a strong smell of urine. It was a dreadful place. Mabel wasn't short a few dollars.

She spent two weeks there, and in that time, Greg visited her just once. Being a married man, he did not offer to take anything there that she may have needed or to take away any soiled clothing to be washed. Therefore, my conscience gave me little choice. I felt obligated to help my fellow human beings, which let Greg off the hook. I was aware of this and began feeling angry with myself for interfering in Mabel's life. My emotions were fluctuating.

Mabel was very particular about cleanliness and neatness. Everything had to be just right. I was learning a lot about being old. I finally persuaded her to let me take some items of clothing home to be washed. I knew she was proud and even somewhat embarrassed to ask me. She knew her personal care should have been her family's responsibility, but they had made themselves scarce in her life.

Meanwhile, Fred had started up about the trash bins again. Both he and his wife sang out the window of their house, sounding like chipmunks, when they saw me taking Mabel's trash down to the gate. I stopped, realising they were making fun of my good deed. They assumed she had me running around and felt I had fallen for it.

"Hey, why don't you come down here so we're on eye level, mate?" I shouted angrily. I was all ready for them.

They came down, both babbling frantically at me.

"Shut up," I said. I just stood there glaring as I let go of both bins of trash. "What's your issue with me?" I smelled strong alcohol; it almost knocked me over. "You're both drunk. You're pissed. Okay, what's on your mind? You think because I'm doing Mabel some good turns, I'm a sucker?"

"We know what she's like," said Fred. "We've been here ten years and seen this before. She's a cunning and nasty old bitch and good at conning people."

I looked at them both, their red faces from being seasoned drinkers. "Let me tell you both something," I said. "I don't give a stuff if she's been an axe murderer. She's an old woman who is physically incapable of taking her trash down by herself; furthermore, I was raised to respect my elders. I don't care what she's done or what she's been in her life. Move out of my way." From that day on, they both showed some respect for me.

I continued to take fresh, clean clothing for Mabel while she was hospitalised. She entrusted me with all her bank affairs and even gave me her gold card, which accessed $125,000 in one of her accounts. Was I tempted to take it? I could have done so easily; there it was in my hot little hand. She had given me her bank account numbers too. How tempting that would have been in the hands of the wrong person, someone without a conscience. I could have conned her out of all her money.

I felt it a compliment that she entrusted me with all her accounts and felt it gave me great power as a trusted, strong, and noble person that she obviously must have thought I was. Either that or she was desperate for someone to trust and felt she couldn't bring her family into the matter for reasons I still don't know to this day, nor was I really interested.

She may have quietly thought me a simpleton for doing what I did for her. Once she was home, not only did I visit her daily, but I also cooked dinner for her at six o'clock every evening. If I was out somewhere, I had to rush to get home, to have her dinner ready on the dot. It was like having a husband who expected his dinner as soon as he walked through the door. It so quickly became a way of life.

Mabel did not expect any of this. I offered to cook her dinner and wash her clothes and sit with her while she churned over the same old stories of her brother who was bayoneted during the war, and her aunt who stabbed her husband with a hatpin in public, and how her father slaughtered the family pet pig for Christmas dinner. Sigh. How I hated having to sit and listen to the gruesome, boring stories repeatedly. Why was I punishing myself like this when I needed so much help? I always found it difficult to leave. In fact, I found it impossible to say, "I'd better be off now." I would finally manage to get away, feeling exhausted and even more depressed.

I longed to be out, smelling of perfume and dressed in high heels, with my long hair flowing in the dusk, gazing into the eyes of a lover over an intimate candlelit dinner, followed by a walk on the beach. Oh, what a fabulous imagination I had when the mundane set in. I took myself off to all kinds of places in my head.

If push came to shove, would I spend my time with a lonely, reminiscing woman who was in her last stage of life, listening to her tiresome and repetitive stories, or would I jump in my car and speed away to meet my lover, who insisted on seeing me on a moonlit evening? My conscience already had the answer. Of course I would stay and listen to Mabel's ramblings.

It got to the point where I had to administer her medication. She even asked me to move into her back room. I politely declined, of course. It seemed I had taken the place of her absent daughter.

Was she that bad? She didn't seem so, but I could see she had been a very demanding woman in her earlier years. I asked myself why I bothered, and the answer was always the same: I might live to be very old. What would life hold for me then? In a sense, this was like looking into a mirror. Who would bother with me when I repeated myself over and over time and time again and my good looks had disappeared? Where would I find love? That thought always scared me.

I was beginning to wish I had not interfered in Mabel's well-being. But I had, so I needed to see it through. Was there anyone as crazy as I was, doing all this out of compassion because I felt sorry for her? Or could it really have been something to do with me and not Mabel? I had to dig deep within my own truth for the answers. Was I in some sort of denial and feeling that if I did not try to do all I could for this woman at the stage she was at in her life, I would be hauled up by karma? Or was there a real god whose hand would strike me down for not doing the best I could? Do we fear reprimand?

I once carried guilt around for not being a good mother and partner. A voice snuck up on me from time to time, reminding me of all my horrendous failures, where I felt I had let someone down. I hated that voice. Some days it never let up.

"Why are you running your ass off after this woman? It's not as if she's even family. She has her own. Make them take responsibility," the voice droned at me, challenging my conscience to the point where I suddenly realised I had gone too far with this woman already. I wanted to back out. How was I going to contact her family? The voice in my head was right: I was an easy touch, and Mabel was playing on my vulnerability. What I had thought had been a few good turns for someone had become a full-time job. I had turned into her carer. Was I too compassionate or was I trying to justify something deep within that I was not quite aware of yet? This needed serious thought, and I knew I had better begin by digging deep and asking myself some hard questions.

I Had Forgotten Someone

My whole world had become Mabel, my mother, and working into the evenings, trying to obtain the money we had lost in our investment. I was forgetting the most important person: *myself.* Compassion had turned into ridiculousness. I was exhausted and running on autopilot. I made a good amount of money, yet it seemed to be going nowhere, as if on a treadmill.

Two days passed, and I had not been to see Mabel. On the third day, I discovered she had not been taking her medication. I felt fed up and wanted all this to be over. My needs were really suffering. I sighed and forced a smile. Finally I had had enough of being the Good Samaritan. I decided it was time to call Greg and make her family take responsibility for her.

When he arrived, I explained everything to him. His wife informed me that she had made meals for Mabel in the past and she had thrown them in the trash. I felt infuriated. She had never thanked me once. I didn't get my money back when I paid for her new commode, yet I could have so easily extracted $125,000 from her bank account when she had entrusted me with all her private details. I clearly saw that my efforts were all in vain. Mabel had never really needed my help in the first place. In fact, I realised she was quite okay left as she was. Seeing her miserable, lonely, bent image through a window, I had taken it upon myself to think she required my assistance.

It had not been my eyes that had deceived me but my guilt and my feelings of unworthiness. I never felt as if I could do enough good, and somehow I had a deep-seated feeling that I owed people. Finally I had realised I owed myself the compassion and time that I was giving out to Mabel. I wasn't seeing myself; I had virtually become invisible.

When I had seen Mabel through her window on that first night, the person I really saw was myself. We are so blind to ourselves and our needs. Growing up, I had been made to feel useless, bad, small, and unworthy of being alive. I hadn't realised I had pushed myself on this quietly independent woman, and when she had failed to thank me and pay me back the money for her commode, I felt offended, used, and angry. I needed to be doing for myself. I had been helping the wrong person.

A Happy Ending

Mabel was soon placed in an upmarket nursing home. She met a man and never pined to come home to her townhouse. I put a call through one year later to enquire about her, and she was happy and settled. I guess I could say she lived happily ever after in God's waiting room with her new soul mate. It was a beautiful end to a wonderful beginning for me.

Lessons Learned

In the meantime, I have witnessed others doing exactly what I did, only with their friends and family members. Women especially seem to be fall guys for the guilt trip, feeling so unworthy that they forget they too have existences of their own that need nurturing. We have been conditioned as women to put the needs of others before our own.

Among the personal lessons I learned from the Mabel experience was that I wasn't the person who was okay. Mabel was quite okay. I was struggling with guilt due to my overall feelings of unworthiness and being devoid of self-love and respect. I wasn't really trying to please anyone, only to quench my feeling of unworthiness.

Some people are people pleasers. They often have difficulty saying no. This is born usually out of fear of repercussion and conflict. They also are not good at standing their ground. They will say yes when they want to say no and then go away and kick themselves quietly in a corner.

Then there is the point scorer—the one who wants to be noticed and gets high on accolades. You know, that type of person that everyone goes to for advice, and then she tells all her friends how great her family and colleagues thinks she is. Some may even whinge to their mates on the quiet about how much they do for their families and friends. They will run the gauntlet for others when it's not necessary, racing themselves ragged at the expense of their own needs. That's also true for the attention seeker. Remember, if we are going to do something for someone, do it and expect nothing in return. It pays to be mindful of what we do for others, whether they're family, friends, or, as in my case, a total stranger. It can add to our guilt and workload and keep us in self-doubt, and we may end up short-changed, without a word of thanks, which can cause us to spiral.

Self-Bullying

Bullying isn't just happening in schoolyards, workplaces, and homes. There are different forms of bullying, including self-bullying. This has been overlooked by a society focused on bullying when there are two or more people involved. An individual is made up of several characters, enabling him to have conflicting and contradicting aspects to his nature, and through contradiction, we often become our own bullies. However, when we love ourselves, there is no room for self-bullying; moreover, contradiction lessens. We become sure-footed on our paths. Self-love is the acceptance of who we are and what we stand for as individuals.

Some never break the cycle of abuse downloaded from their childhoods. They will either learn from it or carry it on throughout their own lives, adding others to their misery list as they go. Those who are desperate to change their pattern strive to obtain the opposite results, not wishing to live out their upbringing, while the rest may simply carry on the violence and obscenities of it. These are the people we find hard to love or to say anything good about. It seems easier for them to carry on the actions of what they have been forced to live out; therefore, their self-worth is non-existent. It was basically robbed from them at birth. No self-worth means no inner strength, which equals no ability to change their direction, and because of this, they believe for so long that no one cares about them, which can give others the impression that they are selfish, hard, and uncaring. The ones who cannot change their path are tortured souls. Education on self is the only key in solving this issue, and it is not taught in schools. Show love to those you don't think need it, as they most often need it the most.

We are capable of doing everything to ourselves that we do to others, good or not. I was bullying myself over Mabel. She was certainly not to blame for this. I set my stage for disaster, which we both could have done without. I pushed myself into her life, insisting she needed my help, when in fact she had not asked me for it. In our minds, we may think we are helping someone while quenching our guilt-ridden consciences at the same time. This is how we bully ourselves, which causes us to push in where we're not needed or to go the opposite way and do nothing. Humans need accolades. We thrive on them. They are like food and water to a person's very existence.

Chapter 4

The Mirror

I felt I had made so many mistakes in my life that I couldn't love myself. I felt like a human doormat, always helping the wrong people for all the wrong reasons, and I found it difficult to say no. I had compassion in my heart, but it had no boundaries. I did not think before I jumped in; as long as I thought I was helping a person, I went in boots and all, without thinking whom I was helping at the expense of my own needs.

With Mabel, I was in no position to help anyone. My health was failing. I was on the verge of an autoimmune disease. Company crooks had gobbled up all my savings, and my mother was very ill. A voice told me I had to let go of everything. As I looked into the mirror one evening before bed, I felt compelled just to keep looking at myself. After pulling a few silly faces, I really looked at my physical appearance. What I saw could have been anyone. I looked ordinary and somewhat drained.

I continued to peer at my reflection. I began seeing myself as others would see me, and I felt a stranger looking back at me. *Where in my body am I?* A strange wave came over me that I couldn't explain. I kept staring at this person who had become a stranger. I didn't recognise myself. It felt weird, but I kept on looking. I felt a shift inside me, and I felt I had no body; the one in the mirror was not mine. As I continued to look, I slowly went inward, becoming aware of my inner core. I could feel everything this person felt and thought. It was like a whole universe. In that short time, I became separated from my body while still fully conscious.

The compassion I felt for this person looking back at me was overwhelming. I felt sorry for her, seeing her tired face and tragic eyes. I wanted to hug her, respect her, love her, and give her the best life I possibly could. I apologised for neglecting her needs and beating her up because I was angry. She was me. For the first time in my entire life, I saw me as I truly was—as a person of worth, dignity, and compassion for all except myself. I knew I was looking at the one and only person who could change my life, yet this person had been neglected.

I encourage other people to do this exercise and take their time with it. It helped me see clearly who I was and where I would take myself from there. The connection you can make with yourself is truly amazing. If this does not work for you the first time, repeat the exercise until you begin to feel a shift happen. It's very simple.

My entire life took a trip down a different road from where I had been before I had made the connection to myself. The first thing I noticed almost right away was the lightness of being. I was soaring inside. The layers of debris had begun melting away, and I felt my power returning.

I felt free, as I had done once so long ago. I had created this glass prison around me, which I could have smashed my way out of at any given moment; all I'd needed was the knowledge of self-love instead of loathing the person I was, and this would have given me the courage to stop being a doormat.

From that day forward, I began mining my own deep nature, attempting to understand my existence as a consciousness being on a much deeper level. I stopped paddling around on the surface of it all and began to see that throughout our lives, we unconsciously download all sorts of rubbish from our past and present conditioning over the years. For example, consider a ball of energy like the sun, which is whole, and then something comes along and takes pieces from that whole. The pieces then become solidified into separate physical bodies of human flesh and we are born. We enter a material world that has been in existence for many thousands of years.

Religion has governed the earth for centuries, and as a result, a system has formed around it, designed to control the masses. This is a huge part of the conditioning process throughout all societies down through the ages worldwide. It controls who and what we think we are as individuals by grouping people into categories, thus taking away our birthrights. For example, in the 1960s, a person was once ostracised for being left-handed and, like myself, was forced to write with the right hand. It was seen as a disgrace and a sign of a person who had not been properly educated. The horror of having my left hand tied behind my back would today be seen as a despicable way to treat a child of five, yet the stigma of being left-handed still sticks. You only need to attend a sports day to hear derogatory terms such as "goofy-footed," "southpaw," "cack-handed," just to name a few still being thrown around in various aspects of sports. The world is definitely an unfair playing field due to conditioning of young minds and governments keeping their people in Third World conditions. There is enough food and money for every single individual in the world. Beliefs stemming from religion are key to our conditioning, whether good or not, and they affect how we see ourselves and judge others. In my quest to seek the truth, I have found that religion sparks fear in those who take it up. It has nothing to do with God, who does not sit on a golden throne waiting to throw us into fire and brimstone. God and religion are separate entities.

"The kingdom of God is within you." We are all God, the life force within, knowing and believing that we are tremendously powerful. Life is not separate from us; it is who we are. Once I understood this on a much deeper level, doors within me began opening. I thought I knew myself, yet I didn't. We can go for decades never opening the door in the basement downstairs, thinking there is only junk and rubbish down there. The person who eventually searches for the key to that basement room will go in and begin poking around amongst all the discarded old bits and pieces and come across something very valuable that changes his life. He comes away not only with a knowledge of what's down there but the bonus of finding something that he never knew was there simply because he had not bothered searching deeply enough. It is the same with ourselves; we do not know who we are until we have opened every door within our inner spectrums. I never knew I was an artist until I opened that door within. Our answers lie with God, that life force of who and what we truly are at essence. "Search and you will find." This is what it really means to search for God—within the depths of your true soul. Search and you will find the kingdom of heaven. We are it; we are the universe.

The Ballard of Being

Lying in the darkness as I do every night, I know there are many people I talk to that I will never see, and the folk I once played and danced with have gone away to another world without me.

Mirrors reflect a frail and much older person looking back at me. It can't be ... but it is—it's me. Where have I gone? Did someone steal me?

Beauty has many faces; it's secretly rooted deep within. We may allow others to pull the roots out of our souls so we once more shrivel and die— black to iron grey, smooth to rugged in its daylight awe. Life like the sea bashing its great self upon me as I wait for it to caress me gently after the storm. On and on through the decades, its relentless harmony of mundane voices still echo.

I am now shameless upon the sunsets, the rain, and the turmoil of life's elements that once pounded my young soul, forcing me to ride it as I slashed at it with wanton passion and a gleaming sword. Ebony hair and eyes as sharp as a razor, the lightness of being on every step. Scoffing at death.

The mirror has not changed. I just appear different. My faithful sword of youth is now a stick, its past and strength hidden from the world except for me. I know the truth.

I am beautiful in a different way now. My strength is stoic, whereas it was once wanton and angry; my hair is iron, whereas it was once ebony; and my body is comfortingly strong in its more frail appearance, where it was once vainly so.

I wonder if I can make my final journey home. I would like someone to come and get me. The tracks of time have overgrown my homeward path.

This world is beautiful, unfair, and tragic. There is no negativity or positivity in the arms of reality. It just is.

Chapter 5

Signs of Forgiveness

I had known Kate all my life—we were joined at the hip—yet it sometimes seemed as if a dark shadow were present like a third person she brought with her. I never quite knew Kate, even though we had grown up together. She had lived down the street from me, and both of us began school at five years of age, on the same day. After our mothers dropped us off and left, I ran after mine, calling and screaming out for her as she hurried down the long dark corridor, her high heels clanking on the old wooden floorboards and her lovely blonde hair scrolled perfectly in a French roll, with a cream fur coat wrapped around her like a movie star. I bellowed for her to come back, fearing I would die in that place of dark doom.

After I had calmed down, I saw Kate. She took my hand and squeezed it tightly as she said, "I'll be your friend forever. Don't be scared." From that day onward, we continued to be the best of friends. We decided to make a pledge to become blood sisters, as we saw them do in western movies, where the Indians would cut their wrists and hold them together, allowing the blood to mix. The scars would be there forever as a sign that you had a true blood brother."

We had planned to do this so we could become real sisters. I took a knife from our kitchen drawer, and we snuck out through the back door of our house to a secret park not far away. I handed Kate the knife as we pledged our sisterhood to one another. Then she cut her wrist. It began bleeding. I then took the knife in my left hand and cut my right wrist, there was blood everywhere, and we laughed with excitement as we held out wrists together tightly until the bleeding had stopped.

Neither of us had thought how dangerous this was. We had no idea that people cut their wrists in order to commit suicide. We were so innocent living out stuff we saw in movies. I still bear the scar on my wrist to this very day, but it is so faint that you need a magnifying glass to see it.

Kate and I were now blood sisters, and that was as good as the real thing. She went to live in England as a teenager, and we kept in touch with letters and cards, until the connection began to dwindle. Time passed quickly, and months turned into years before I would see her again.

I eventually lost contact with her whereabouts completely. I decided to track down her brother, who was still in Australia. He remembered me from years ago. I wrote to her in England. It was months before I had a reply, saying she wanted to attempt to come back down under. I was over the moon. I offered to pick her up from the airport.

In the days leading up to her arrival, I started becoming fidgety, wondering if she would still be the same as she was all those years ago. But why would she be? That was over forty years earlier. She called me before her flight. She spoke so affluently in a Queen's English accent, making me feel rather uneducated, my accent echoing into the mouthpiece. "Crikey, she's come a long way," I mumbled gently, putting down the phone. Her voice and accent had changed.

I had taught Kate to play the piano jazz style, without music sheets, when we were at school together. We both entered a competition, and when she won, I felt as if an invisible arm had pushed me backstage, out of the limelight. I had taught her all I knew about music. I was to learn later that she had taken her music career further and become a classical pianist who played for an orchestra in London. I had certainly been left behind.

Feeling inadequate, a small voice came into my consciousness. *Rikki, you were the instigator of the path in which Kate chose to walk. All those years ago, she looked up to you. You loved each other. You bonded in the blood of sisterhood under that big oak tree in the park, and that is what has stayed within the subconsciousness of both your minds. You gave her a precious gift, and that was to inspire her to become who she is now. It is a result of a step you put before her, which she built her life upon.*

A stream of light came into my body and soul. I almost immediately felt as light as a feather. It all fell into place. We often don't know who we have inspired, and their lives can change because of it. I couldn't understand why my own life had not moved ahead yet Kate's had with gusto, and then I began seeking the reason I had neglected my own path.

The day came when Kate was to arrive in the middle of a Queensland summer. The heat would get up around forty degrees Celsius most every day. My thoughts raced as I got into the car and began heading towards the airport. *What will she think of me now after all she has achieved in her life?* I couldn't wait to get this part of it finished. I parked, got out, and strode into the main entrance. I sat tapping my right foot nervously. Suddenly, she appeared. I slowly rose out of the chair. She looked just the same except her hair had turned iron grey and was long like mine was. She was lean and lovely. I hurried over to her, saying, "Kate." Her head turned in surprise. She looked straight at me, and we hugged long and hard. There were a few seconds of awkward silence before we both burst out in nervous laughter.

There was no need for words. We headed for the car and then to a cafe before going home. We instantly picked up from where we had left off all those decades ago, and the conversation effortlessly flowed. There were no awkward moments. I looked down at her wrist when I thought she wasn't looking and saw the vague scar of our childhood pledge. To anyone else, it would have just been a scar, yet it felt strange seeing it on her now mature arm.

We arrived home at around dusk. I had left the lounge light on, and we flung ourselves down on the big red sofa. "I'm going to have a coffee. How about you, Kate?"

"Yep, count me in for that." I was aware of how differently Kate spoke with her lovely accent. I did not yet know the reason for her coming back to Australia after so much time had passed, and I was dying to ask.

"So are you staying for good seriously, Kate?"

"Yes, I have a container arriving by ship in three weeks from England."

"Oh God, really?" In my enthusiasm, I punched a cushion. Kate just sat looking at me.

"Oops, I'm sorry, Kate. I got carried away." I placed the cushion nicely back into place again. I felt silly and awkward at my childish outburst. I had momentarily forgotten that we were not children anymore.

Two weeks passed wherein we were getting on famously, but there was something wrong with Kate. She would often sit outside, gazing down at the grass, occasionally lifting her head wearily at the sound of a fleeting bird. I felt she didn't want to be disturbed. As the weeks continued to pass, I noticed pauses in her behaviour, almost as if she were hiding a secret. Kate had never had children - perhaps this was why she seemed to want to be by herself at times. I had to pick the right moment to ask her more about her life. I heard the door open, and in she came.

"What's up?"

"Huh?" she said.

"You know, where are we going out to eat tonight?"

"You pick."

I chuckled. We laughed hard and fast, sounding like two kookaburras, just like old times. I thought my chance might come that evening at dinner to find out what secret she might be hiding.

Kate was in good spirits, and I wondered if asking her about her past would be such a good idea. It could upset her and ruin our night. I had to see where things went.

Arriving at an Italian restaurant, we sat and ordered our meal in a Santa Fe atmosphere of Tuscan hues. The deep Italian culture had long fascinated me, and I longed to visit Florence and Tuscany. I'd had these questions on my mind for the past week, and that's all I could think of at dinner, waiting for my chance to see what was haunting this lovely woman.

"Kate," I said.

She immediately shifted her glance, looking me straight in the face. She continued staring bright-eyed, waiting for me to say something. I suddenly felt this was not the time to ask her about her life. My mind went into overdrive as her gaze continued. I felt slightly awkward, hoping she didn't suspect I was dying to ask her.

"Um, have you been to Italy, Kate? I've always felt a strong pull towards it. For some reason, I feel that I was born in the wrong country."

"Nothing wrong with being born down under, Rikki."

"I guess not. It's just that ... I feel so unrefined when I speak, and I have always been self-conscious about it. Mum always used to say to me, 'Rikki, you're beautiful until you open your mouth.'"

Kate began giggling, spilling some wine on her dress. "It's true, Kate. People expect me to have some sort of fancy accent to match my classy appearance, and I just don't. Makes me sad." We both fell into fits of uncontrollable laughter, which drew attention from some of the surrounding tables.

"Maybe you'll get to go to Europe with that lovely man you've known all your life."

"Not all my life Kate—only the past thirty years."

"Well, that's almost a lifetime, isn't it?"

"Yeah, I guess." My perfect chance had come before the conversation inadvertently changed its direction. "Speaking of men, Kate, you never mentioned marriage or children. I take it there aren't any, are there?" I could see her mind ticking over. "Whoa, sorry. We don't need to go there if you're not comfortable."

"No, it's fine, Rikki, really. I never married and have no children; my entire life has been spent working." Kate looked down as her long fingers twirled the stem of her wine glass.

"Had you wanted marriage and children?"

"Honestly, no. I have to say that I've never longed for it."

"Kate, I've noticed how you become distant at times and for long periods, and I confess to thinking that this may have made you sad."

"No, not at all Rikki."

"What do you work at nowadays, Kate? Is it your job making you seem sad?"

"If I tell you this, you'll hate me forever." She raised a shaky hand to cover her mouth, screwing her eyes up. I felt I was putting her under pressure, yet I knew she had a deep secret she had to get out, one that was holding her back. I could not even begin to guess what was so bad at this point. Had she accidentally murdered someone? I was beginning to brace myself for something horrible.

Kate began sobbing, and I knew it would get worse; she was ready to let this out now, right here, and it drew attention from nearby tables.

"Let's head for home, Kate. You can make that famous hot toddy—you know, the one with the whiskey in it." I winked and gave a slight chuckle.

I grabbed my bag and Kate's coat, and we left. The silence was deafening on our ride home. Kate's eyes were red-rimmed and glassy. She seemed to be almost traumatised. I had to figure out what was wrong, which had been my intention practically since she arrived.

Once inside, the sound of the jug revving up felt comforting. I put on the soft red lounge lamp. We both huddled under a thick sofa blanket, top and tail. Kate was sipping her toddy while starring at the coffee table. "Crunch time, chick." I was gulping down mouthfuls of coffee, wondering what her first word would be.

"I don't know where to begin." She began sobbing again.

"Start anywhere, Kate. Just get it out. Have you murdered someone or something?" I'd said it jokingly, but her whole body went limp, her head buried into the arm of the sofa as her body shook. *Oh God,* I thought, *she has killed someone.* I sat motionless, waiting for her to stop sobbing. "Kate, you must tell me, please."

"It's not a joke, Rikki. I am a murderer."

"What?" My mind had gone blank.

Another coffee for two coming up, with whiskey. Lord, how I needed it right now. Kate sat up straight as I handed her another drink.

"Rikki, I haven't been a good person. I'm an evil and horrible monster, and I don't deserve to even live another day."

"What on earth do you mean, chick? It's me you're talking to—Rikki. Remember when we cut our wrists all those years back when we were only kids. On that hot, sunny afternoon when I handed you that knife, we were so excited." I grabbed her right wrist and placed it over mine, holding it tightly. "Blood sisters—that means for life. We still bear the scars. There's nothing you can't tell me, Kate. You have to tell someone eventually or it will break down your life and destroy you. If you can't tell me, then who will you tell?"

"Promise me you won't ask me to leave. Oh God, have mercy on my poor ignorant soul."

"I would say, Kate, that whatever I'm about to hear, it would be more like your *innocent* soul speaking." I was becoming more curious as to what this was all about.

"Rikki, I worked for four and a half years inside an animal testing laboratory. It was horrible. I had been out of work for a very long time, and my mother got me the job. I had no idea it was a place where they murdered innocent animals, until I had already taken the job as a cleaner there."

"So let me get this straight, Kate. You worked as a cleaner, which meant you were no part of any experimentation groups, correct?"

"I was employed to clean inside the laboratories, but the people I worked with were all lab technicians. They were nice to me and treated me very well; in fact, they would include me in everything, never looking down on me because I was just the cleaner."

"What about your music career? Where did that finally go, Kate?"

"It was my music that kept me going. I would work all day at the lab and play a concert twice a week, sometimes on a Saturday evening. You gave me my first platform, Rikki. If it hadn't been for you, I would never have had a music career."

"Nonsense. Of course you would have, with or without me. It's in you, Kate. You've got it. Now go on—tell me more about this joint."

"I was twenty-three when I went to work there. It was in the basement, below the ground floor. There were no windows. There were UVB lights in every corridor to take the foul smell of urine and death away, but the smell was still very pungent all through the place. I found it difficult at first. It took three months for the smell not to bother me as much. My job consisted of scraping out cages full of woodchips, urine, and dried faeces. I would put on a long green gown, a cap, and mask, along with gloves. Rows and rows of empty cages were stacked up to the roof. I even dreamed about them. I became very adept at my job. All of the waste was scraped into huge brown paper bags, which I tied on to three funnels, so when one became full, I would move on to the next one, then staple them up tightly. The bags would then be loaded onto a huge trolley, which the men would come and take away, along with the dead bodies of animals.

"I would then proceed to line the cages up on huge racks to be sterilised. The machine made a hell of a noise, and the room would fill with steam, which contributed to an even gloomier deathlike atmosphere under the cold fluorescent lights. It was anything but a glamorous job, yet I became used to it."

"Did you ever feel like quitting that terrible job, Kate?"

"Well, you see, it wasn't that terrible because people respected me, and after I had worked there for three years, they offered me a complete promotion to upgrade to a lab technician."

"So at that point, you believed that this type of a promotion was an upgrade. An upgrade to what, Kate, to actually take part in murdering animals in the name of science. Is this what they call a promotion, a license to kill?"

I noticed Kate's chin begin to tremble. I already realised she was deeply saddened by her past, and I toned down on her. Time for another coffee break.

"I don't want to talk about this anymore. Let's have a break. Tell me about your life over the past forty years, Rikki. I know you never married."

"How could you know that?"

"Because you were so adamant that you would never end up like your mother."

"Oh, you have an extraordinary memory, donaordin. Kate laughed aloud as I moved towards the open pantry. "Men have always found me too challenging, I have to say, and not a bit sissy. They seem to love my complexities, yet that's what drives them away from me eventually. I have no idea why they bother. Strange, isn't it?"

"Hmm, yes. I met a man in the orchestra in London. The very first evening we went for dinner, he wanted to know how I became interested in classical piano. I told him the story of us and how you taught me to play jazz." I laughed, thinking how sweet that was.

"I was learning classical piano, as you remember, and my piano teacher and my mother were both horrified when I became bored with having to practice every day after school for two hours. I hated playing classical. I wanted to play jazz. In fact, I was determined to do so. I turned my classical pieces into jazz format, without the need for music sheets. I was wrapped over the knuckles and sent home, and that was the end of my piano tutoring. I was free to play jazz until my heart was content, and I loved it."

But, Kate, you went on to bigger things after that. You owe that to yourself, not to me."

"I don't see it like that, Rikki. I wanted to be just like you."

This time I laughed with slight embarrassment. I was desperate to hear more involving the laboratory. "Kate, are you feeling okay to continue on about life in the animal labs. Where did we get up to?"

"The cleaning of the cages."

"Yes, of course." Pausing to collect her thoughts on this terrible venture once again, she said, "I remember the stray cats sent in from the local animal shelter. Their heads were sliced open, and microelectrodes had been placed into the gaping holes in their skulls. Some of them just sat in one place, their eyes looking at me as if they had given up all hope of anyone coming to help them. Others paced up and down, hoping for a way out that was never to be. Their only way out was death.

"The animal testing laboratories were down in the basement of the building. There were four floors above: pathology, psychology biology, and dentistry. These departments all tested on animals. The cats and rabbits were there for the psychology scientists. The rats, mice, and hamsters were used by pathology and biology technicians, as were the sheep and dogs. The basement layout consisted of a huge main surgery that was like a big operating theatre, with two smaller surgeries off the main one, used for sheep. All the laboratories were situated around the big main surgery. Oh, how I hate that place. The memories of it still haunt me to this day. I need coffee."

Rising up off the sofa for what felt like the tenth time, I hobbled into the kitchen and flicked the jug switch. My leg had gone to sleep, and I was feeling drained from listening to such trauma. It was after two in the morning. I felt for both Kate and the poor animals who had suffered at the hands of so-called science. I began to feel angry at her. Why didn't she make her music a full-time career? All these random thoughts ran through my head as I stood with my hand wrapped around the handle, feeling the vibration of the jug about to pick it up.

"May I ask you what made you keep working in such a place?"

"I don't know. You see, at that point, it didn't bother me. As time went on, the more it seemed to eat into my soul. We are conditioned to believe that animals have no souls and don't feel pain as we do. As I got older, I went down a path of self-growth, seeking my purpose to life. Pain is pain. It's just what it is. It's felt by every living being as something that is as unpleasant as what we know it to be. Pain is not something that another being feels that is different from the meaning of the word itself, as we humans understand it. It is not one thing to us and something different to an animal. Pain is consciousness, as is joy, and it covers the whole consciousness spectrum of being. It is knowing and being aware of an experience, whether pleasant or not. And in this case, those animals were terrified and bewildered and made to suffer loneliness and great pain, all in the name of science. Animals are no different from us; we are all connected as one through consciousness.

"Kate I know something of the deeper meaning of life, and that is it pure and simple. This was your lesson, as hard as it was, and all the time I had thought that was what was making you so unhappy was because you had never had children."

Kate's face broke into a smile as she placed her hand upon mine. It was nice to see a glimmer after such a gruelling few hours. I had no idea animals were treated so cruelly at the expense of cosmetics and cures for human beings. I felt disgusted.

"What made you leave that gruesome job, Kate?"

"I fell pregnant …"

"I thought you …"

"I had a miscarriage."

"Oh, shit. I'm so sorry you went through all of that on top of the job."

"As I said, the people were nice, and the money was even better."

I felt a harshness in Kate's voice, making me take a step back. It was an instantly awkward moment. Was she guilt-ridden or feeling sorry for herself? I had to dig much deeper to find an answer.

"What was the worst thing you ever saw in that laboratory, Kate?"

"I saw heaps of things that would make your hair stand on end, and I won't tell you."

"Why the secrecy?"

"It would do you no good to know."

"I think I can guess how bad those laboratories are. I think it would do you some good to tell me. It will help you to get it out. I'm all ears."

"When the dogs were brought in, even the most vicious of them would become frightened and shake with fear and disorientation. They knew they were in a place of death and horror. I remember this one in particular, as it was my job to hose out the pens that housed these dogs.

"I got close to this one, and he growled loudly at me. He was not like the others; he was proud. He never took his eyes off me. He stared me straight in the eye, and I felt a shift take place within me. Suddenly, it was if the blinkers had fallen from my eyes. I stood for a moment just looking at him; he continued to glare at me. I moved slightly, and he growled again. One of the lab technicians broke the silence. One of them asked me to help him with this dog, to heave him onto the weighing machine. We then placed him in a cage. He continued to look at me, his lips curling with a snarl. How he hated me. This one dog had stood his ground on his own, despite the fear he felt, knowing his fate.

"The rabbits had chemicals in their eyes, some of them in tiny cages. Some were totally blind, crashing into the bars trying to escape. They performed vivisections on cats and rabbits with no anaesthetic.

"Inside the laboratory, small animals were bred especially for the purpose of testing, like the nude rats. They had no thymus glands. These were tested on to establish the effects of different types of drugs used in cosmetic surgery. I would go in to mop, and they would be coming out of anaesthetic. They were full of radioactivity, and they hobbled around with their eyes running and half-closed. Their backs had been stapled up, and they shook. I could see they were suffering the worst pain I have ever seen, and they were kept alive only to die slowly and painfully after they were of no more use. I want you to know, Rikki, that the place I worked in has haunted me for the past thirty or so years. One of the worst times was when we had the medical students come down over a four-day period. Dogs were brought into the main surgery and cut open. Sometimes they didn't use anaesthetic and you would hear screams echoing down the corridor and into the tearoom.

"I was under oath, not permitted to tell anyone about it. I could never bring friends or even my family members to the animal testing labs. There were signs up to stop the public from going in through the doors. I came to work one day to find that animal activists had managed to get in the place. We were all quickly grilled on what to say if caught off guard and confronted by any of the media while going to our cars after work. The activists had written all over the walls of the medical school. I had no idea what an animal activist was back then. I was so ignorant of so many things, Rikki. You have to believe that. I have never touched an animal in any way I should not have. I was asked by a technician once to hold a dog while he euthanized him. Ten seconds after the needle went in, the dog gently rolled over in my arms. Peace had come quickly at last.

All the while Kate had talked it out, I had listened. "What happened the day you left?"

"I worked up until one month before having the miscarriage. They offered me a position if I decided to return to work as a technician in a specific-pathogen-free—SPF—unit, a term used for laboratory animals that are guaranteed free of particular pathogens. The use of SPF animals ensures that specified diseases do not interfere with an experiment. I left the laboratory and never returned. I can't get my life together. All these years, the terrible guilt of not doing anything to stop animal testing has gnawed at me continuously."

"You didn't do anything wrong, Kate. You simply did a job, and people in those days responded to their conditioning. No one knew any better. We have all been conditioned to subconsciously believe that animals don't feel pain as we do. Please … You must stop this blaming of yourself. You can't take on the world; you didn't create it.

"Does is bother you because you might go to hell if there is one? I always believed that hell was here on Earth."

"I don't know what to believe anymore. I only know that I can't live with this awful guilt. I didn't take action. I should have done something to try to stop this. In the back of my mind, I knew it was damn wrong."

"Kate many people go their whole lives through and never wake up. At least you definitely do have a conscience, and that stopped you from going back to that job. You may not have even been aware of that at the time."

"You always have an answer, Rikki. Where does that all come from?"

I shook my head gently and shrugged. "I think about things, Kate. Every six months or so, I stop everything just to settle within my own consciousness, and I begin to ask myself if anyone is suffering because of the way I'm living my life. I also ask myself what I can do to improve my quality of life and if I can do anything to help others improve theirs. In other words, I self-check to see where I'm at in life, and I am continuously updating it. It's like taking your car in for servicing. I take myself in for a six-month service to ensure I'm keeping ahead of what I need to in order for me to keep moving slowly forward."

"How have you helped others?" Kate's voice lifted as she shuffled herself, sitting up straight, ready for the big one-to-one seminar. I felt that what I was about to tell her, she may already know.

"I don't directly set out to lift people, Kate. It happens by making a conscious effort to keep self-improving. It seems to speak for itself. I would like to think of myself as some sort of guru, seeing people look up to me."

"Really, Kate."

"I think I feel a coffee coming on—no, I'll just have plain water instead, I think."

"So your ego tells you this, Kate?"

"Huh?"

I felt Kate becoming agitated at my challenging little question. "You say you would like to be a guru and have people look up to you. Is this all you want, for people to look up to you?"

Kate realised what I meant, and I could plainly see that she felt uncomfortable. We were taking things out of our comfort zones and beginning to get to the essence of life. I was feeling quite accelerated.

"Kate, forgive me for speaking as I see it, but I do feel you need to face your demons before you can even begin to try to help others. You help number one before you can be an example to anyone else. Your path to self-growth and development is a lifelong commitment, and besides, it doesn't work as you think it does."

"What do you mean?"

"I mean that you need to deal with your issues. They are the demons within your subconscious mind that are holding you back from moving forward with your life. You need to get rid of them, Kate. Yes, the laboratory you worked in has to be dealt with and put in a place within you where it cannot affect your present and future life. You can never erase it from your mind, but you can move it to a place within you where it won't be able to hold you over a barrel."

"I want to ask God for forgiveness, Rikki. Do you think that's a good way to start? Do you believe there is a god?"

I was unsure how to answer her, and knowing I had to be careful with my reply, I gazed down at the carpet for a moment before looking up at her. "God is within every being that lives and breathes—animals, humans, and insects. Even the wind and wild thunderstorms are pure energy that is cosmic energy.

"The kingdom of God is within you, which is your consciousness, and it's your choice to be happy. People have many names for this, Kate. Some call it the higher self, while others mny call it the universe or a state of grace. Consciousness is awareness and knowing. We cannot touch it, smell it, or hold it, yet we know it is there. This has nothing to do with religion of any kind, yet many religions base this state of grace upon being godly. Don't tell me you still believe that old rubbish about some super being wearing a crown of light on his head, sitting on a throne, waiting to send you to fire and brimstone." I chuckled roughly.

"No, of course I don't," said Kate. We began laughing, and it felt like old times again.

"Hey, Rikki, I know you've never been one for religion, but how can I ask to be forgiven for all the wrong I did?"

"Wrong? Who said you're wrong, Kate? You did what you did then. If you had actually known better at the time and continued to work in that place of death, then you would have been committing a sin—or in my words, a moral crime—but because you didn't know any better, it was just a job you did. Again, we have been conditioned for decades to believe that animals are lowly creatures of a lesser echelon than what human beings are. We all believed that rubbish at some point in our lives, yet sadly many people still believe this because they are uneducated on the higher levels of what their purpose truly is. But times have changed, Kate. You're going back to the beginning of the nineteen eighties, when women were just beginning to grow wings. We believed we couldn't fly, making us codependent on others. We naturally believed what we were fed from the time we were born, until our consciences tell us to listen to the truth. This is your conscience seeking the need for forgiveness.

"You're not a bad person, Kate, nor will you go to hellfire," I scoffed. "That's a myth, and I have my own doubts about the way karma works. We live in a world of threats. If we don't pay our bills on time, we're threatened with penalties. If we fall sick and can't get into work, we are threatened with not receiving pay or having to make up for lost days, whether we feel up to it or not, and any time for holidays is always hanging in the balance, along with the uncertainty of job loss. We are consistently being beaten over the head with threats and shadows that embed into our psyches, affecting the way we think and perform."

Kate put her head in her hands and let out a huge sigh "You always have a way of making people see things, Rikki. How do I rid myself of this terrible guilt? It won't go away, and it's horrible."

I knew that whatever I was about to say could affect her more than anything else could right now. She was confiding in me and seeking the truth; therefore, my answers had to have merit. "Kate, I am not judge and jury, yet I have evolved enough to admit that I honestly don't know what happens when we die. We are not meant to know, for if we did, people would turn it into a money spinner, and they already have to a degree. I don't know, Kate, but one thing I am sure of is that the universe, or God, is within us all. We are like mini gods. Our minds are powerful beyond belief, and this is what makes or breaks us. I have a quote that has taught me that we are responsible for our choices. *Life is partly what we make of it, and the rest is what we allow others to make of it.* No gloss, Kate. It's just the way it is. We need to understand the reasons for existence on a greater level to truly know who we are, without being influenced to waver by others. We can only achieve this once we make our choices and operate through a higher level of consciousness. It's like taking steps until you reach that point where it becomes a part of your life. On another note, how's your music career going?"

"Oh, it's wonderful. I owe it to you, Rikki."

"You owe me nothing, Kate. You went on and took it further. I only gave you the first few steps." I smiled shyly at her.

"Why didn't you keep your music going?"

I took a deep breath. "I don't know. I guess I just couldn't settle down. Other things in life distracted me."

"You mean men?" Kate nudged me.

"Yeah, blokes, as they say down under." I rolled my eyes. Mum wanted me to become a classical pianist. Remember Dad's collection of jazz records? I had always wanted to play jazz. I love the sound of offbeat disc chords; there's something wild and free about it. My mother was horrified at that, so I kind of lost interest in piano after being forced to keep playing classical. It seemed too rigid and just didn't fit who I was. I wanted to express myself with more gusto, and having to read music sheets made me feel restricted. I guess it wasn't in my blood. I mean, don't get me wrong, Kate. I enjoy classical music, but it can also make me feel very sad. I never told my parents this. Jazz, on the other hand, made me come alive. I don't know why classical has this effect on me.

"My father didn't care one way or another about anything I did. He was never home, he always had affairs with other women."

"I remember all those parties up in the attic at your house all those years ago. The island dancers and the music, and your father was always drunk …"

"Yeah, that was him, always pissed as a fart." Kate burst into great laughter at my casual outburst, and again we both went into fits of laughter, throwing cushions at one another like children. The laughter slowly subsided, and we were both quiet. Kate propped up on one arm as I lay with my head resting on the opposite arm of the sofa, gazing tiredly at the wooden beams on the ceiling.

I knew there was more to come out of Kate. She was someone who had carried a great weight on her shoulders for decades, and it needed to be lifted. I know she wanted to hear me say there was a god. I had to try to get her to feel that god force within her own being before she could let go of her guilt. I had to be tactful in my approach to this. She somehow thought I had the answer because she believed I was responsible for her career as a classical pianist. I had learned something about life and motivation: no matter who you are or what position you're in, you have the ability to make someone's life better. You do not have to be doing anything great yourself in order to give others the encouragement they need in order for them to build steps to their own success. This was apparent with Kate and me. Here was I, having lived a life of rebellion and thrown away a music career, and all the while, Kate had taken those little steps I gave her earlier and had apparently built her entire life on them. I needed to realise that I was special in the same way Kate was. I had somehow managed to do this for Kate instead, and that made me feel extremely worthy. We were friends on the highest level. The bond we had was inseparable. Even after thirty-odd years, we could still play like children and laugh aloud at ourselves.

"If it's any consolation, Kate, there's nothing to forgive. You have not harmed any animal in your years of working in that place."

"I know, Rikki, but I was there. I should have done something to stop it."

"Why don't you ask for forgiveness, Kate? You need to rid yourself of this weight in order to move on."

Kate nodded her head." Yes, I want to do this tomorrow and get it over with."

"Right. Tomorrow in the backyard, sit in a chair and ask God to forgive you."

Kate's face lit up a little, perhaps at the thought that I may secretly believe in a super being sitting upon a golden throne after all.

We both woke to the sound of kookaburras laughing. We had fallen asleep on the sofa. Kate stirred and groaned at the noise of the birds and the light peeping through the crack in the curtain. I got up and flicked the switch on the jug for coffee. This was the day that Kate was to let go of her past, the obstacle that seemingly had held her back for decades. "Coffee, madam?" Kate began waddling out towards the kitchen. She looked pale. I handed her the hot mug. "Today is the day, my friend." Kate sat idly; the only sound was her sipping her coffee. "I'm off for a shower. See you in a tick, mate." I headed down the hallway, whistling tunelessly.

After showering, I came out to find Kate gone. I looked in the bedrooms and outside, and she was nowhere to be found. I called, but there was no response. The car was still in the garage. I went back outside and around the house, calling her name, but Kate had vanished. It was out of character. I began thinking the worst. Then suddenly I heard a loud bang—the screen door had slammed shut—and dragging of footsteps. I rushed towards the sound to find Kate wearing a pair of my flip-flops. "Where have you been?" I cried.

"Out walking. I don't know how you wear these things every day. They hurt my toes."

"That's because you have delicate English feet, my dear. I never wear shoes unless they're open styled and I'm able to just slip them on."

Kate giggled.

"God, woman why didn't you tell me you were just popping out for a bit? You had me worried."

"Thought you would have guessed."

"Let's go eat." I grabbed the car keys. "While you're here, you can practice walking in those flip-flops. You're dragging your feet in them, old girl." She watched me as I slipped my feet into a casual pair of open white scuffs that had a small heel. "After we've eaten, I'll take you flip-flop shopping."

We headed down the highway for a girls' day out. Having Kate here meant I could take time off my projects and cruise for a week or so. I was enjoying the company, and my impulsive buying excited Kate. As usual, I overspent and bought stuff I didn't really need, which was half the fun. I had always been impulsive and never tamed this part of my nature. It had free rein. It never did anyone any harm, except burn a hole in my own back pocket occasionally. Life is for living and giving to oneself. No one should feel guilty about spending money on themselves, and I never have. I am as deserving as anyone else of gifts. Many people only buy for others, only for items to end up in preloved clothing boutiques, or thrown out after having hardly been worn, or just left in a corner somewhere.

At least when spending money on myself, I have purchased things I really love. Can't beat self-purchasing; it can become an addiction.

Finally arriving home worn out from shopping, Kate tried on a pair of white shorts and open shoes to match, a couple of items she had found in a bargain bin. "My legs are lily white; I'm so pale. I should have bought some instant tan, but I was too distracted by all the colourful bling in the shops. Wow, I love the coast."

"Me too. It's spoilt me for wanting to live anywhere else but here. You know I've always been a tropical fish type." Kate continued to absorb herself in the mirror, admiring her new attire. "Looking good, chick, white legs and all."

She slapped me gently with a coat hanger. "I'm ready for my meeting with God. Do you think he'll like my new attire?"

"Don't be silly. What would he care? Besides, what makes you so sure *he* is not a *she*?"

"Don't know, really. It's just something that automatically came out of my mouth. Most people refer to God as 'he.'"

"I don't."

"That's because you don't believe there is a god," Kate remarked.

"I didn't say that. Remember our talk last night. I said that God was within us. I believe in a higher being. Many don't realise this is a part of ourselves we don't recognise. Yet we have been conditioned to believe God is separate from us." I felt I had said enough; the atmosphere was becoming touchy. "Your beliefs are your personal choices Kate, I don't have any right to tell you what you ought to believe in" Feeling heat on the horizon, I quickly changed the subject.

The day had passed quickly, and it was already late afternoon. The temperature was a high of thirty-eight degrees on the sunny Gold Coast of

Australia. The clouds looked stormy, and the birds had ceased chattering in the trees. Often we experienced an afternoon summer tropical storm that gave off an eerie feel. "I'm going outside to have my little conversation with God!" Kate called from the bedroom. I heard the screen door close. Just before I sat down to my computer, I peeked out the window. Kate was sitting in my lonely chair with her eyes closed. I could see her mouth moving slightly.

Time flies when I'm on my computer. Over an hour had passed, and Kate had not come in. I peeked out the lounge window and into the backyard. She looked peaceful and happy, and I didn't disturb her. I was hoping somehow her prayers would be answered.

The phone ringing broke the silence. It was another telemarketer. I shouted down the phone at him, banging the receiver down, mumbling aloud, and swearing into thin air. Kate heard me, and she came running in to see what I was swearing about, forgetting about poor Kate enjoying the peace after her important personal ordeal. I felt selfish and apologised to her with a hug before I proceeded to ramble on again about nuisance phone calls.

"Calm down, chick. My word, you have a short fuse. That hasn't changed, has it?"

I knew I looked rather sheepish, and I felt somewhat silly at my big outburst.

"Have you ever tried an anger management course?"

"Yes, twice—and both times I came away more angry than ever."

"You really should work on that, Rikki. Your stress levels will go through the roof."

"Yep, I know Kate. I just can't rein it in. It just comes out. I can't explain it. It's part of me, and people just have to accept the fact that I don't tolerate certain things."

"Oh, yes, like telemarketers."

"That's it, Kate. Don't try to work it out."

At times, Kate's perfect Queen's English made me feel rather inadequate, especially losing my cool over a silly call that meant nothing. I loved Kate all the same.

Kate had to return to London in four days. I began feeling heavy. I didn't want her to leave. Both of us wanted one more week, but it was impossible. She had concerts to attend back in London. "Next round is yours, chick. I'll show you London. You'll love it."

"Yeah, the double-decker buses … They always look as if they're about to topple over."

Kate reassured me with a friendly pat. "Oh, you'll be all right. You need to see Europe."

"I want to see you play in a live orchestra. I wish I were going back with you."

"Then why don't you?" I felt tempted. Perhaps I could, just for a week, to see Kate perform. The excitement grew inside me.

Kate didn't have to say much more to convince me to go back with her. I immediately booked my flight to London online. We became like children again, hitting each other with pillows and laughing. That was what was so special about our friendship. We would often burst into extreme excitement and be totally crazy chicks. "Nothing like doing random, aye, old girl?" she said.

"Yeah, booking a flight with a crazy friend to the other side of the world … That's challenging my comfort zone."

Two days later, my mother drove down for the day for lunch. After having a relaxing time outside, Kate came in, collapsed on the bed, and fell asleep, I noticed she had a slightly pinkish tinge to her skin from the harsh Australian sun. Mum was sitting in a deck chair under a palm tree. I hopped on my computer while I had some time to myself.

The sound of Mum's voice pierced the quietness; I rushed out the front door and into the backyard to find her pointing. I looked down by the gate, and there was a beautiful chocolate-coloured rabbit. He had appeared from nowhere. Rabbits are illegal to keep as pets in the state of Queensland, and there are no wild ones. I instantly knew he was friendly. I went over towards him, and he allowed me to pick him up with ease. His coat was soft and shiny, and he appeared to be well cared for. But where did this awesome creature come from? Mum and I were astounded. He had just appeared as if he had fallen from the sky.

Kate heard the commotion and came out to see what all the fuss was about. Her mouth dropped open, and she covered her face and gasped. "This is the answer to my prayer. Oh, Rikki, I asked for a definite sign," Kate cried with joy.

"What?" said my mum. "I don't understand."

"Never mind, Mum. I'll explain later. This is not just a rabbit."

Mum looked so confused. "You two are as mad as March hares. I'm going inside for a cup of tea."

"Tell me, Kate." I nudged her with my arm.

"There is a god, Rikki. He answered my prayer. I begged for forgiveness from the Almighty for turning a blind eye to the horrific suffering I witnessed when I worked in the animal laboratory, something that had burned me up inside for decades. I asked that I also be forgiven by the animals themselves, and I wanted a sure sign of it."

The universe had heard Kate's words. I feel that she had forgiven herself through prayer and a wonderful manifestation had taken place. I felt happy for her. Finally she could move on in her life. But what were we to do with a rabbit that was illegal to keep in Queensland? I had never seen so many pebbles come out of an animal in my entire life, so we named him Pebbles. We had to keep him inside until we figured out a plan for him. We decided to put him in the laundry; it was quite large, with lots of room for him to move around. We grabbed blankets and I picked up some hay from a local stockfeed outlet.

We kept him for two days while I finally located a friend in another state of the country where it was legal to house rabbits as pets. She ran a sanctuary for rabbits, and as luck would have it, she was coming down this way the next day. We met at a nearby gas station and dropped Pebbles off. He was soon adopted out to a loving family.

All was well. Kate had been shown a sign of forgiveness, and I was going back to London with her the next morning. I couldn't wait to hear her play. I was almost beside myself in anticipation.

I had never been on such a long flight. I became agitated being confined with people coughing and bored children screeching. I certainly was no seasoned traveller. When the time came to touch down, the landing was smooth and the skies were grey. My body clock was out of kilter, and I had a slight headache. Once we were out in the fresh air, I instantly felt a chill, and the rain was so icy cold that it almost felt like hot pieces of flame attacking my skin.

"Man, it's cold," Kate said, and I felt a little silly. Suddenly, I wanted to turn and get back on board the plane. I had never been to Europe, and already the change in climate had begun affecting me in strange ways. Kate hurried to a nearby cab. I seemed to be running short steps to keep up with her. I wasn't used to wearing heavy coats and shoes on my feet. The city of London appeared to be gloomier than I had imagined. The old architecture was fabulous, however; I had never seen anything quite like it. The immensity of its history overwhelmed me. "You'll get used to it before the week's up, old girl."

I nodded with a silly half smile. "Remember, I've never been to Europe."

"So what—nor have a lot of folk."

"Yeah, I guess," I mumbled into my woollen scarf.

The taxi pulled up outside Kate's apartment, which appeared old, yet there was something deeply nostalgic about it; it brought back a feeling of something I wasn't quite sure of. Perhaps it was a dream I once had of London.

I woke the next morning to the sounds of the neighbourhood awakening, doors slamming and engines being started up as people went off to work. *It goes on, the same old pattern*, I thought, lying there warm and comfy. Kate's apartment was quite stylish in an oldish way, with high Michelangelo-type ceilings. A partly broken chandelier hung from it. Both the walls and ceilings were the same colours, a greenish grey that had faded, yet it gave character to the place. The carpet was off white with a large worn-looking mat in the centre of the floor. A lovely distant view of London could be seen from the lounge and both bedrooms. Artwork of European painters hung in gilded frames. They appeared noble. England was the home of many great artists and writers. The curtains were beautifully draped in large seashell pleats of delicate faded apricot. This was so different from where I had come from back down under. I couldn't possibly walk around in flip-flops here. My feet would freeze, the poor things. I just adored Kate's apartment. Although London was smoggy at times, it was nice.

Tonight was the night I had been waiting for, to see Kate playing in the orchestra. We rode a double-decker bus around the city that day. I was constantly aware of the cold and feeling the need to keep ducking into cafes for hot drinks. "How much more coffee can you drink, Rikki?" I didn't answer as once more we quickly headed down a narrow lane.

"Hey, wait up, chick. What's your hurry?" I could hear Kate's footsteps running behind me.

"I'm running out of the cold, Kate."

"Is it really that bad?" We were both puffing, but even running didn't seem to be warming me up any. We stumbled into the door of a cafe and ordered two big mugs of hot chocolate. London was great. It was humming with energy that reminded me of a colder version of parts of Sydney.

After taking a few gulps of the hot stuff, I felt my body tingle and thaw out, and it felt good.

"What have you done with yourself all these years, Rikki?" asked Kate.

"Where do I start?" I replied in a ho-hum manner. "Life has been all over the place, Kate. My relationships have all failed. I backed the wrong horses, I guess." I laughed.

"Why didn't you take your music further? Your dad was a great clarinet player."

"Yes, he was, Kate. That's where he met my mother, in a dance hall. He had not long been back from the war. She would catch the ferry boat to go to the dances in town every Saturday night, and my father played all around town. She caught his eye, and it went from there.

"As you know from way back, all I wanted was to be able to play jazz music; my mother was disappointed. She was all for classical."

"Yes, I do remember her making you practice every day after school, and you would begin turning classical into jazz."

"Yeah, I know. Poor Mum. I put her through ghastly hell." I put my head in my hands, and we began to laugh.

"Oh well, the music world just wasn't for me, seriously. I managed to play a couple of nightclub gigs, but that was about it. Smoky clubs never were my thing." We were warm and relaxed, and Kate gazed at me with a faraway look, as if she had so many deep questions she wanted answers to. I didn't know where to begin, as my life had been a tragedy/triumph of regaining my true self-identity, which had taken all my good years. How could I tell her this without her feeling disappointed in me?

Life had certainly taken me down lonely and empty roads over the years. Kate had remained stoic in her decision to follow her dream, and I had fallen. Oh, yes, I had dreams, but the hand of fate had gotten to them before I could make them real. Can we entirely blame ourselves for the choices we make? After all, we have to live life, and making choices it is all part of being alive. We do the best we can at any given time. That's what I did. I had concluded that I had not made mistakes but gained knowledge through experiences that had made me stronger and compassionate, even empathetic. What is important is that we learn from our experiences, good or bad. It's like marriage—you have to take the good with the bad and roll with its punches.

"You know, I truly enjoy our conversations about life and its deeper meaning," said Kate.

"Me too, Kate. I'm writing a book."

"What—really?" she said with surprise. "Aha, a love story ... It would have to be with all those jokers you've known."

"C'mon, Kate. Give me credit for having a brain. Why would I waste time writing about those wankers?" I shook my head with a smile.

"Tell me about some of these wankers." Her English accent made me giggle. I then laughed uncontrollably. "What's tickled your fancy now? I only asked about the wankers in your life." She began giggling as well. We both ended up paralysed with laughter and tears running down our faces.

"Promise me, Kate, that you won't say the word wanker," I blurted out through the laughter. "Sounds so funny coming from you." After we had both calmed down, Kate looked at me, red-faced and teary-eyed. "Are you going to tell me about those you-know-whats?"

"Can it wait till tomorrow? I can't wait for tonight's concert."

Kate glanced at her watch. "Oh, we'd better go, chick. Concert begins in two hours, and I have to be there an hour before it starts."

We took a red double-decker bus back to the apartment. I was feeling nervous about the concert, yet I would only be an observer in an audience. *Why so uptight?* I asked myself. Could it be that I was going to be shocked that her life's progress, which would show me how undernourished my own life had been, was making me feel like crawling under the nearest rock? I felt apprehension in the pit of my stomach.

The time had come. Kate called for a taxi to pick us up from her apartment. The traffic was thick. "Don't you get anxious before your concerts, Kate?"

"Just a little." She seemed to conceal it well. I was becoming fidgety in the taxi, and I wanted the evening to be over. I was more anxious about Kate's performance than what she was. The taxi pulled to the left and continued up a narrow driveway to the back of the theatre. We got out, and almost immediately some people came walking over to meet us. Kate seemed very comfortable in their presence.

"Fellow orchestral members, Kate?"

"Why, yes, I want you to meet them all."

It was warm inside, and I could hear the echo of violins and cellos behind the din of people talking. Off long corridors, I saw musical instruments in every room. I had never experienced anything like it in my life. This was England, the home of poets, artists, musicians, and writers, and Kate was in her element amongst it. She was excited about showing me around and introducing me to everyone. I found myself almost running to keep with her as she strutted down the corridor, farther into the depths of the theatre.

We came to a piano room. "Go on, have a bash."

"Good God, Kate, not here."

"Why not? No one can hear you. Everyone's busy getting ready for the concert. What is it? You look as if you're about to cry."

"Kate, I'm a jazz pianist. You know how they rate in the classical world. How embarrassing."

"I want to hear those songs you played me when we were children. I wanted so much to play like you, I was so envious."

"Yeah, but that was then, Kate. I'm not a real pianist. I've forgotten how to read sheet music. I play by ear." Kate was dragging me by the hand

and pushing me to sit at a perfectly tuned grand piano. "I suppose you're going to tell me you have never played on a grand?"

"One or two times in my life." I was feeling nervous and very out of place. I was afraid to put my hands on the polished keys. "Oh, get into the swing, chick. The thing won't bite you."

Nervously I began to play "Summertime." I had no audience other than Kate, yet my hands were shaking. I could hear the distant din of voices and instruments practising way down the corridor in an organised manner. I closed my eyes and transported myself back in time to a hotel in Auckland City, where I used to play the odd gig and had been requested to play the song "Summertime" on many occasions.

Surrounded by a haze of cigarette smoke in the dim light, with glasses clanging, people sometimes shouting, and police raids in those days, I began vamping out the old-time song, only aware of the scene in my head as I continued to play for what seemed to be hours. A crashing sound broke the momentum, and I opened my eyes to find people clapping and whistling. I was stunned and embarrassed. Kate walked to me and took my hand. I stood up and bowed to my small audience as Kate spouted about how I had been her childhood inspiration. Everyone shook my hand, and I was invited backstage once more after the concert was over.

Masters and Mistresses

It was time to head off to my front-row seat in the concert theatre. I was early and sat contemplating the events that had taken place earlier that evening. A middle-aged man came along and sat beside me. "I always go for the front-row seats," he said in a fine English accent.

"Me too," I replied softly. "I'm here to watch my best friend perform tonight."

"Really? Are you Australian?"

"Well, yes, but I'm originally from New Zealand. I've lived in Australia for a long time."

"How interesting. It's not every day that I meet someone from New Zealand or even Australia." I grinned at his remark. "Are you living here now?" No, my friend whom I've come to see lives here permanently." I showed him her name on the concert program. He seemed insistent on talking to me. I was a little relieved when the lights dimmed and the orchestra began coming out. He had at least taken my mind off the nervousness I'd had been feeling about the evening.

His head turned to look at me in the dim light. "By the way, my name is Earl. I'm sorry—I should have introduced myself before the concert began."

Pointing toward my shoulder, I replied, "Rikki. It's quite okay, Earl. Nice to meet you."

I was finally here at last; it had come, the night was about to begin. Kate had told me earlier that she was going to do a solo part. As they began playing, I waited with bated breath for her solo, and then confidently her fingers ran the over keys so quickly without a mistake. I was amazed. She must have practiced for hours a day for years, while I was friggin' around with useless men on the other side of the world. I wanted to cry over my wasted life, but Earl was sitting right there.

"Isn't she brilliant?" he whispered.

"Yes, she is—very much indeed."

"People who play in orchestras are usually inspired by someone, either a great musician or someone in the family," Earl said. "I'm really not sure who inspired Kate. Perhaps you'd best ask her yourself afterwards."

As the night progressed, I began wondering if I had really been her inspiration. Perhaps she would have pursued this path even if I hadn't been in her life. No one would ever know the answer to that. I was thinking of telling Earl the story, but then, he was a stranger. I was confused. One part of me felt good that Kate had been so inspired by me in her childhood, yet another part of me felt it was a personal injustice to take the credit for where she was now. Perhaps Kate thought I had inspired her and was unaware that she would have still pursued her music career, regardless of me.

I wanted to know what an outsider thought. Interval had arrived, and the lights had been turned up. Earl asked me out into the foyer for a cup of coffee. It did not seem to be the ideal time to go into this; I had only just met the man. "Would you prefer a glass of wine instead, Rikki?" I laughed. "I don't mean to be a bore, Earl, but I think I'll give the wine a miss tonight."

"Coffee it is, then." He took my arm gently and escorted me towards the atrium, where he pulled a chair out for me.

My gosh, he's a true gentleman, I thought. My mind began running away, and I wondered if he was married. He was moderately handsome, lean, and tall. He had obviously been well educated. His hair was honey blond and parted on the left side, and a strand sometimes dropped over his brow. I had an urge to gently push it back off his face and run my fingers through his thick hair. I found his boyish Clarke Gable appearance charming. He was a breath of fresh air. I would have guessed his age to be around forty-five. His hands were manly, and I noticed he was not wearing a wedding ring. I suddenly remembered that I was only in London briefly and scheduled to fly back to Queensland the next day. I was looking forward to the warmth and getting around in light clothing and bare feet once again.

"You look stressed," said Earl.

"Oh, it's nothing. I've only begun to get into the swing of things here and I have to fly out tomorrow. Gosh, how time flies when one is having fun."

"Can you not extend your stay?"

"No, not without quite a bit of juggling. It wouldn't be worth the extra dollars." Oops. I suddenly realised that was a rather insulting statement to say to a lovely gentleman.

"I'll pay the extra," he said.

I was beginning to feel awkward, and I felt that my distrust of men was becoming obvious. I made light of Earl's remark. "I would love to stay on, but I can't. I have to get back to Australia. I have projects hanging."

I knew he was going to insist. He had that "I don't give up easily" look about him. I was ready for it.

"You're extremely attractive, and I like your personality," he said.

Hmm, I had heard this so many times over, like a broken record. I looked away, making out that something had taken my attention, and pulled a face at the air, rolling my eyes. I completed his sentence in my head. Yep, here we go again. He probably wants a gap filled in his life and I come along. Perfect timing, Rikki. You're good at this aren't you?" I looked towards him again. The old familiar agitation I knew so well returned; it never quite goes away. Someone always brought it out in me repeatedly. I lightly patted his hand and gave a laugh." You're too kind Earl."

"I'd like to know more about you."

"Like what?" I replied in an aloof manner.

"Everything."

"Where do I begin?" I said, staring down into my coffee cup.

"Anywhere."

"Okay, may I begin here—about tonight, the reason I really came to London?" His head tilted slightly. I could see that he was ready to listen to me talk, but we had to return to our seats in the theatre.

"Rikki, would you accompany me for a late supper after the show?" he asked.

"Well … I've been asked to go backstage after the concert." I felt awkward again. I wanted the chance to tell someone about my true reason for coming to London, but at the same time, I couldn't let Kate down tonight. Perhaps she wouldn't mind if I brought Earl backstage. Oh God, I was not good at dealing with such social awkwardness. I thought the best thing to do was be honest.

"Earl, there's something I would like to talk to you about, but I don't think we're going to get the chance tonight and I have to be on a plane early tomorrow."

He placed his hand on my shoulder. "Tell you what," he said. "Why don't I come visit you in Australia?"

My heart raced. I knew this meant a relationship, and I was nowhere near ready for it.

I was in a dilemma in my head. I decided to take Earl backstage. *I know Kate's going to think I'm up to my old usual tricks with men again and that Earl had topped her performance on stage,* I thought. *I know what she's going to think. I wanted the chance to talk to this man, and there wasn't the time. This has been the result of everything in my entire life. Misunderstandings and bad timing. Kate will not see it this way. Do I agree to him visiting me in Australia?*

I dealt with the problem directly and took him backstage after the show had finished. Thank God I had met this man, as he had taken the sting out of what may have been a sudden depression for me with the impact of Kate's success. Yes, she was so successful, and I would appear to have never moved forward. She was brilliant.

We walked down the dark hallway of the theatre. With all the confusion in my head, I had forgotten where I was supposed to meet Kate. It was a huge place, so I decided to ask someone. The person pointed us in the direction of her room. As I opened the door, she came out. We banged into each other.

"Kate." I hugged her and told her how amazing and brilliant she was on stage.

She stood without uttering a word. "Oh, Kate this is Earl ..."

"Harris," he said extending his hand out to Kate.

I hadn't known Earl's last name. I knew this whole thing would make me feel idiotic and cheap, as if I didn't feel bad enough about my wasted life already, but this was different, only Kate didn't know that Earl had been sitting next to me as a complete stranger. It was just Rikki up to her old boyfriend tricks again, I guess she thought.

"Chick, Earl happened to be sitting next to me at the concert."

I know she didn't believe me. I could see it as she walked past us and closed the door, her eyes fixed on us both. Earl seemed to sense this too, and he intervened with a great explanation that seemed to calm things down. He invited Kate and me to a late supper.

When we got out onto the street, I felt the cold night air stinging my eyes, and they began to water slightly. Earl seemed to know where the best places to eat were, which made me think that perhaps he got about with the ladies quite a bit. If a man knew all the great restaurants in town, then he was sure to be a ladies' man. There went my wayward thoughts again.

Kate seemed to be quite taken with Earl and that was understandable, for he was charming, witty, and spoke like a gentleman, with manners and looks to equal.

He went ahead and opened the door to a quaint little place with a fire going in the corner of the room. It contained low sofas, and paintings graced the walls, along with bits and pieces of English history that had been generously framed. I loved the historic atmosphere of this place. We ordered a meal and some drinks. We talked shop for about half an hour, and I was hoping to get a chance to have that conversation with Earl, but time was running out. I decided to work my way around to it. I didn't mind talking with Kate present. I had nothing to hide. I wanted only to quench my burning desire to know if I had truly inspired her enough to make music her career.

"I'm so proud of your performance tonight, Kate. In fact, I'm proud of you. I'm glad I made the effort to come to London."

"So am I," Earl chipped in. We all broke into laughter. I took a sip of champagne, held it up, and we had a toast to the future, a wonderful evening, and many more concerts to come. Clang get went the glasses.

Silence followed. *It's now or never,* I thought. "Earl asked me earlier what inspired you to become a concert pianist, Kate."

"So did you tell him?"

"No, I didn't get a chance to really, and I thought you could tell him."

Kate began telling Earl about our lives as young children back in New Zealand. Earl insisted on seeing the scars on both our wrists where we had cut them to become blood sisters. He seemed fascinated by all this. "If I had not met my best friend, I would never have gone this far with my music studies to become a concert pianist."

"Oh, I see," he said. "You two are most interesting ladies, to say the least. I feel I have known you both all my life, yet we have only met tonight."

"Odd, isn't it?" I said. "Life is a mysterious carnival of dreams and coincidences. I'm sure we live all our lives down here and don't even need to die to have all these different lives. We change in appearance and find we have actual capabilities we never thought we had. Life is like chapters in a book, changing and growing, exploring and finding."

Kate and I were feeling tired. It had been a big day and an even bigger evening for us. Earl looked as if he could run a marathon, and I could tell the night was still young for him.

"Time for a taxi, Kate?"

"Yes I need bed too," she replied. "Earl what will you do the rest of the evening?"

"Oh, probably find a late night movie to go see. Would you like to accompany me?"

"You mean both of us? Rikki might, but I'm dreadfully exhausted and must go home." Oh no. I too was so tired; I didn't have much stamina, and the whole London thing had really taken it out of me.

"Thanks for a lovely evening, Earl. I hope you can get out to beautiful Australia one day." Kate went on ahead to hail down a taxi. Earl gently paused with me as we headed out the door. I turned to face him. "You are quite the warrior, Rikki."

"That's odd, Earl, because my background is Polynesian and European, and I've always been called a warrior-type person."

"I had been wondering if you maybe have a Spanish or Italian background. Your skin is that lovely biscuity colour, and your eyes are dark and smouldering," he said. "My father was Maori, and my mother is European. I'm a half-caste." Earl told me how the Haka (Maori war dance) frightened him but he loved its power.

"I guess I'm a fighter, Earl, more or less a survivor. I will fight for the underdog and those I love; that's sacred to me. Sadly, my father and I never got along. He has passed now."

"I'm not surprised. The two of you were probably the same. I like you even more now."

I laughed. "Please don't make fun of me."

"I meant what I said. I like you a lot, Rikki, and I would like us to be good friends." "Thank you, Earl. Perhaps we can write via the computer." I handed him my email address and phone number.

"You gave Kate her inspiration to continue her career as a concert pianist, Rikki. This is how I see it because it is so very obvious."

"What made you say this, Earl? Are you humouring me?"

He placed both hands on my shoulders. "No, that I'd never do. I see the power you hold within. It's in your voice, your eyes, the way you hold yourself … You're different from anyone I have ever known. You are proud yet kind, strong but not of steel. It struck me when I first spoke to you tonight at the theatre."

"Earl, not now, please. I have to return to Australia in just a few hours, and its already gone midnight." His eyes searched my face; I felt his fear of never seeing me again. "You can call me and email me anytime. He smiled with relief.

"I know I can trust you, Rikki. That's what I meant. You are like no one I have ever known in my life, and I want to see you again."

"We'll catch up soon. This time you can come to my cafe down under." He bent slightly and kissed me on the cheek. I knew he wanted a proper lovers' kiss, but this time I had to be sure of his motives. I never played easy to get. Perhaps he was genuine and wanted sincerity. I was always sceptical of a man's motives.

We parted outside the restaurant. I got into the taxi, looked back, and waved to Earl. He blew me a kiss, and I blew one back.

On the plane flying back down under, I felt tired and somewhat wretched. My eyes felt as if someone had thrown sand in them. I ordered a glass of champagne to relax my body. The gentle erratic turbulence caused me to drift off partially into a twilight zone. I began dreaming. I could hear noises around me, yet I was somewhere in between worlds. Earl's voice was clear as if he were next to me. I jumped, only to find an empty seat with my cabin bag on it. I finished my warm champagne. Again I partially floated into a twilight zone, only this time it was Kate's voice I heard. "I would have died if you had never crossed my path years ago. It was your letters, emails, birthday cards, and most of all my admiration for being yourself even at the cost of losing people who never saw your true worth anyhow. So much of you has rubbed off on me. I found compassion through what

I saw you doing for others. Those years I worked in the animal laboratory, I remembered how you used to save caterpillars and ladybirds.

"I longed to play jazz piano, but my mother—like yours—insisted I stick to classical. Only you rebelled and followed your heart with jazz because you weren't frightened by your own light. I wanted so much to be you."

"Excuse me, ma'am," a voice said. I was instantly pulled away from Kate. I sat up from being partially slumped in my seat. "Would you please fasten your seat belt? We're about to land." I grappled with the damn thing, feeling slightly annoyed at the inconvenience.

Once we landed, I sat in my seat until the bulk of the passengers had gone. I had a dull headache accompanied by tiredness, but I knew it would go away as soon as I got out of the plane and into some fresh air.

My London trip had me thinking. Deep down, I still wondered if Kate's life would have taken her into a music career if we had never met. Based upon what she and Earl had said, perhaps I had helped her make that final decision to pursue her passion and success. I yawned and stretched before getting out of my seat. I felt animated, and it gave me a good feeling to know that my trip to London had been a success. The bonus was that I came home sure of my measure as a person. My mission had been accomplished in that respect and in meeting a charming man, which didn't turn out as I imagined it would. I was so negative about him to begin with.

I had every right to feel good about myself. It dawned on me that even though I had not pursued a musical career, I had given Kate many reasons to fulfil a passion that otherwise may have lain dormant for the remainder of her life. I am glad we met and became blood sisters. I still believe in magic. As I headed home from the airport, I received a text message. I checked my phone, and there was a message from Earl. Oh God, he had already booked a flight out to Australia and would be arriving in four days' time. The chase had begun. I knew I was keen on him; I just didn't want to allow myself to be vulnerable again. I put my phone in my handbag. I happened to catch my own glimpse in the rear-view mirror of the shuttle bus, as I was sitting directly behind the driver on the right side.

I had a smile on my face, and my olive complexion was aglow. *Gee, you're a hot-looking mama*, the voices in my head told me. I kept looking at my reflection in his mirror, until the driver caught on. I quickly looked away and out the window. I had four days to organise my villa. I began to imagine what it would be like to live with Earl and share my life with him. Would he expect marriage, which was something foreign to me? To take another person's name … I couldn't imagine being anyone else but me.

I had to be me. No one was ever going to make me someone else and give me another name just for the privilege of spending my entire life with him. What did it matter, anyhow? I was not about to marry the man, and the random thoughts in my head would more than likely go nowhere.

When people say, "I don't know where life is taking me," it will give fate its chance to step in and create a path for them, for better or worse. If we have no direction in our lives, then the universe will step in and create one of its choice. Grab your wheel and take control of it.

Life is energy. It is fluid and lucid and can be moulded by its master or mistress, which is ourselves. We are all hardwired to compare ourselves to others around us without even being aware of it. This causes jealousy and unhealthy competitiveness, whereby we can waste so much of our precious time competing with others on the level of the green-eyed monster.

However, a certain amount of jealousy is a good thing. It's one of life's main motivators. The downside is that jealousy never seems to stay in one place. It grows, and we need to be well aware consciously that once it takes over our lives, it becomes unhealthy and turns into a monster.

Feel the edge of jealousy and leave it there. Don't cross over the edge. I speak about jealousy because it is such a powerful emotion that resides in our DNA, and if used correctly, it can get you the life you want. Most of the gurus will tell you that jealousy, anger, and fear are negative emotions that you should cast out of your life for good. This is only because no one has actually come up with a way of knowing how to channel these emotions. It's rather like peeling potatoes and throwing away the skins simply because that's what we have been conditioned to do with them.

The skins actually contain all the nutrients. In other words, like jealousy, anger, and fear, they are the best part of your make-up and can be channelled just as potato skins can be used to make nutritious soups and be combined with other veggies. These powerful emotions are part of who we all are in the big picture.

Today's society tells us that if we feel joy and happiness 24/7, then we are doing it all right. Society is totally unequipped to deal with jealousy, anger, and fear; therefore, those are things that we should shun instead of deal with. There are so many courses that try to teach people how not to be angry, fearful, and so forth, while suffocating the best parts of our natural power along with it. Where there is light, there will be dark, but we are only taught about how to thrive in the light by getting rid of the dark. Night/day. Black/white. Joy/ fear. It is all simply a process of life itself.

I realised that I would have to talk deeply to Earl on his visit. He was coming out to see me with obvious intentions. Was I ready for a relationship with a man who lived on the other side of the world? He may want me to live in London. Perhaps I would live there for a few months. I was getting ahead of myself. Would I feel the fear and do it anyway? This was one quote that truly made sense to me whenever I read it anywhere. Headlong into a relationship, how would he cope with my mind. I had not been an easy challenge for men in the past. If he could not cope with my entirety, then he was not the man for me. I had to remind myself again that we are all masters and mistresses of life.

I am.

Printed in the United States
By Bookmasters